Victoria and Albert Museum

Homage to Kokoschka
Prints and Drawings
Lent by Reinhold, Count Bethusy-Huc

London 1976

Acknowledgments

Count Bethusy-Huc wishes to thank the following for their heart-warming enthusiasm and generous friendship, which have contributed so much to make this exhibition a memorable one:
Dr Wilhelm F. Arntz, Haag in Oberbayern
Dr Bernhard Baer, Richmond-on-Thames
Gotthardt de Beauclair, Mandelieu, France
Hans Bolliger, Zürich
Frank H. Dickinson, Dunedin, New Zealand
Professor Gottfried von Einem, Vienna
Dr Ivan Fenyö and his wife Dr Lenika Fenyö, Budapest
Professor Sir Ernst Gombrich and Lady Gombrich, London
Dr Lisbeth Gombrich, Oxford
Erwin Heidrich, Vienna
Professor Dr Carl Georg Heise and his wife Hildegard, Hamburg
Dr Wolfgang Henze and his wife Ingeborg, Campione
Madame Edith Hoffmann-Yapou, Paris
Professor Edgar Horstmann, Hamburg
Miss Christina Huntley, London
Miss Lesley Jones, London
Professor Dr Otto Kallir, New York
Florian Karsch, Berlin
Dr C. M. Kauffmann, London
The late Professor Bohuslav Kokoschka and his wife Minna, Liebhartstal, Vienna
Professor Dr Oskar Kokoschka and his wife Olda, Villeneuve
Dr E. W. Kornfeld, Bern
Professor Ernst Křenek, Palm Springs, California
Hermine and Erich Kreuzer, Schikaneder-Lehar Schlößl, Nussdorf bei Wien
The late Dr Gustav Künstler and his wife Dr Vita Maria Künstler, Vienna
Sara and Robert Learmonth, London
The Directors of Marlborough Graphics Limited, London
Universitäts Professor Dr Fritz Novotny, Vienna
Dr K. B. Palkovský and his wife Lida, Prague
Meister Karl Peschek, Vienna
Sir John Pope-Hennessy, London
Graham Reynolds and his wife Daphne, Suffolk
Mr H. G. Sedcole, Harrogate
Lady Anima Terpsichore, Eleusis
Dr Jan Tomeš and his wife Helena, Kunštát na Morave
Professor Friedrich Welz, Salzburg
Edi Wolfensberger, Zurich

Foreword

Some years ago, the Museum was fortunate to receive, as a long term loan, the unrivalled collection of the graphic work of Oskar Kokoschka assembled with great expertise over many years by Count Bethusy-Huc. A selection from the collection was shown at the Bethnal Green Museum in 1971 and, when that exhibition closed, any item from it remained available for consultation in the Print Room of the Victoria and Albert Museum, as it will again after the end of the present exhibition.

Meanwhile, the collection has continued to grow and we are now happy to be able to show a larger, more comprehensive selection as a tribute to Kokoschka on his 90th birthday. This book, also, in which we are pleased to publish the work of so many distinguished scholars, is intended as an offering of homage to Kokoschka as a graphic artist and I should like to thank the contributors most warmly for their ready co-operation.

Roy Strong
Director

Contents

Introduction
E. H. Gombrich

In celebrating the 90th birthday of Oskar Kokoschka we are paying homage to one of the great outsiders of contemporary art. Indeed the visitor to this exhibition of Kokoschka's graphic oeuvre may find it difficult at first to locate all the phases of the rich and varied production on his mental map of 20th century art history. He will at once recognise the echoes of Viennese *Art Nouveau* in the early postcards which Kokoschka designed as an art student and in the illustrations to his first book *Die Träumenden Knaben* (The dreaming youths) dedicated to his master Gustav Klimt. He will vicariously enjoy the wild outbursts of creative energy during the revolutionary period of European art between 1908 and 1912 when Kokoschka appeared to be more radical even than the 'wild beasts', the *Fauves* of Paris and became the bogey man of the Viennese bourgeoisie. His subsequent collaboration in Berlin with the *avant garde* Journal *Der Sturm* (a counterpart to Wyndham Lewis's Journal *Blast* in this country) appears to place him firmly in the expressionist movement, but from the twenties onwards the lines of Kokoschka's development refuse to conform to any such frame of reference. Why should a leading pioneer of the modern movement have turned to portraits of cities, how could he become so engrossed with the heritage of ancient Greece which we associate with the academic tradition? What made him lash out against primitivism and abstraction? And yet, the more one studies his work, his personality and his writings, particularly his moving autobiography,[1] the more one realises how much his development is all of one piece. Any apparent inconsistencies should not be laid at his door but must be blamed on the inadequacies of the map.

Perhaps the basic ambiguity arises from the idea of a modern movement in art, for the word modern becomes so easily fused with the concept of progress. Yet the historian knows that most of the intellectual ferment which gave rise to the artistic revolutions of this century sprang from a refusal to accept the myth of progress which had inspired the 19th century. There are few of Kokoschka's utterances in which he does not take issue with the optimistic notion of scientific, technical and political advance. The intellectual ancestry of his ideas can thus be traced back to the Romantics and to such prophetic figures as John Ruskin, for whom the machine became a symbol of spiritual death, an instrument of de-humanised mechanisation which outraged the dignity of man. The gnomic profession of faith which Kokoschka published in 1912 under the title *Die Natur der Gesichte* (The nature of visions)[2] must not be pressed into a philosophical system, but in its emphasis on intuition and creativity it recalls the philosophy of that influential thinker of the early 20th century, Henri Bergson. Like Bergson, Kokoschka exalts the idea of flux against rigidity, of spontaneity against convention, of vision against cerebration.

Hindsight tells us that this revolt against reason had its dire consequences in the ideology of Fascism and National Socialism with their cult of 'blood and soil' and their rejection of the intellect. Kokoschka's passionate humanism, his hatred of regimentation, made him fully proof against this contagion, just as his individualism and pessisism made it impossible for him to join the rank of progressive Utopians. In this independence he was no doubt fortified by the influence of two mentors of his early years, the architect Adolf Loos and the pamphleteer Karl Kraus. Like Kokoschka himself these two prominent figures of Vienna's intellectual scene have sometimes been misunderstood. Their defiance of middle class conventions stamped them as subversives in the eyes of the public, but their challenge was aimed at the progressive Left not less than at the reactionary Right. Loos, whose name has become associated with his polemic against ornament, was really out to attack affectation and artifice in the name of a healthy unfussy craft tradition. Kraus raised his voice against the degradation of man, which he saw reflected in the debasement of language. The butt of his satire was the journalistic cliché and the thoughtless and rootless slogan, whatever side it came from. The denial of sexuality by a hypocritical society was to his mind a symptom of the same mentality which had drained language of its natural life. Mankind would perish through the 'black magic' of printer's ink unless we found contact again with the roots of meaning. It was in this spirit that the small band of rebels which Kokoschka joined denounced the modern age which had violated nature. What form should this movement take in art?

In 1908, when Kokoschka had just burst upon the scene, the German critic and art historian Wilhelm Worringer aroused much attention with his book *Abstraction and Empathy*. The two labels were intended to stand for two contrasting types of art; abstraction being characteristic of all primitive and ritualistic styles as a symptom of the dread of nature allegedly felt by members of the cultures concerned. 'Empathy', that feeling for life we associate with classical and Renaissance art, was only possible for civilisations which had mastered this anxiety and lived at peace with nature. Whatever the rights and wrongs of that schematic theory, it certainly struck a chord at a time when *Angst* was much discussed among artists. The withdrawal from nature in the movements of primitivism, cubism and the various forms of non-objective art implied a rejection of empathy. Seen in terms of this alternative it is clear which road Kokoschka had to follow; his was and remained the road of empathy, of what Albert Schweitzer was to call the 'reverence for life'. Lack of such reverence looks to him like the unforgivable sin against the Holy Ghost.

In the year 1920 at the age of 34, when he was teaching at Dresden, Kokoschka was asked by the anxious father of one of his students whether the young man had any chance of a career in art. Kokoschka's letter of reply which is printed in the artist's autobiography[3] contains perhaps the most succinct formulation of his artistic creed. He did not want to hide the risks of disappointment and of failure, 'but I must not close the door to a person who believes that he alone among many thousands will find the path to what the enlightened call the divine. Indeed as a true teacher I even want to encourage anyone who is ready to stake his life, so that the imagination of the divine should not remain without a priest and life not without the greatness of classical antiquity' (*damit die Phantasie des Göttlichen nicht ohne Priester bleibe und das Leben nicht ohne die Grösse der Antike*). I have added the German because any translation loses the emotional overtones of the words the artist had used. *Die Grösse der Antike* evokes the almost religious awe with which Winckelmann, Schiller and Goethe had invested the ancient world; *Die Phantasie des Göttlichen* likewise reverberates with the ideal of the imagination as a prophetic faculty of which the artist is the priest. Even in his more lighthearted or contrary moods Kokoschka never deserted this conception of his mission.

In this light the inchoate and violent images and writings of his most revolutionary period can be understood as a deliberate submission to the divine power of the imagination. In the years of his adolescence spontaneity counted for most with Kokoschka. He would have found it inconsistent with his ideal to restrain the turbulent intensity of his emotions as they poured forth in his plays and his illustrations. No wonder the public felt threatened and that even his admirers saw mainly aggressiveness in his unconventional portraits. In the first monograph on the artist, which was published in 1913,[4] we read in Paul Stefan's introduction that the 27-year-old painter had become sufficiently established to allow him to create as and what he liked. Stefan interpreted the early portraits as acts of revenge on society. He could not see human beings, 'only beasts and ghosts'. There is such an artist in Ibsen's last play, *When We Dead Awaken* (1900), who claims that his society portraits are really intended as revelations of his sitter's animal nature. The critic's diagnosis was probably influenced by this model, but it was mistaken. Kokoschka's portraits have always been compassionate rather than aggressive. To quote the artist's own words from his memoirs: 'What used to shock society at first in my portraits was what I tried to divine from the sitter's face, the play of features and of gestures so as to sum it all up in my pictorial language as the memory-image of a living being'.[5]

This was and is his reason for refusing to submit to the conventional demands of decorum, but what he finds behind the mask is not the animal but more often the forlorn and lonely human soul. The key to Kokoschka's achievement here as always is precisely his capacity for sympathy. I have tried in a different context to show how he has used his uncanny powers of empathy in this process of psychological exploration.[6] If there is an element of the self-portrait in all his portrayals this is due to the way he attunes his own body to resonate to his model, re-enacting the expressive movements of his fellow-humans so as to understand them more fully. He responds to people as others respond to music. No wonder that one of his most memorable sequences in this exhibition, the *Variations on a Theme*, embodies this dual reaction – that of his model to the changing moods of a work by Beethoven, and that of the artist to her changing expressions (pl. 17).

Responsive though he has always been to great music and great literature Kokoschka has lived through his eyes. Our eyes are the instruments telling us of the incessant flux of life and of light, which make it impossible to arrest nature without killing it stone dead. Even as an art student Kokoschka broke away from the traditional methods of the life-class, in which the model is posed and thus deprived of the sense of life. He asked his models to move freely about the room – a method Rodin was to adopt about the same time. Kokoschka never lost faith in this pedagogic device, which was central to the 'School of Seeing' he ran at Salzburg in the fifties and early sixties. He knows to the full what Max Liebermann has stressed in his beautiful essay *Die Phantasie in der Malerei* (On the Imagination in Painting), that every act of representation is an act of the imagination, for nature cannot be copied, only reconstructed on the canvas. It is for this reason also that he acknowledges with such gratitude the achievements of the great masters of the past who, since the days of the Greeks, created the visual language of painting without which the artist cannot capture, hold and communicate his unique experience. To an artist of this persuasion the visual and the visionary are one, for every image is a creation. Looking at the variety of the artist's graphic productions created during more than six decades one gains the intuitive conviction that none of them – whether portrait, landscape, dream or illustration – would have gained shape if the artist had not been profoundly moved by what he saw with his outer or inner eye.

Kokoschka had sought such encounters on his extended travels in the twenties and thirties when circumstances were more favourable to painting than to print-making. Conditions also varied during the later periods of his life when he continued his nomadic existence less from choice than from necessity, fleeing from Prague to England in 1938, where he remained resident till his move to Villeneuve on Lake Geneva in 1953. Throughout these vicissitudes, however, his art changed but little, for he carries his world in his head. The intensity of his reactions was never blunted by habit or resignation. Reports of callous inhumanity have frequently aroused him to protests in word and image, though he has never had any illusions about the chances of changing human nature. Neither has his deep pessimism diminished his gratitude for what mankind has created in the past and for what life can still offer to those who have eyes to see.

In one of his early manifestos Kokoschka took the *Orbis Pictus* by the seventeenth century Czech educationalist Comenius as his text for a denunciation of the utilitarian outlook.[7] It is not purpose which matters in life but meaning. Perhaps it is this message above all which underlies the response Kokoschka's art has always met with. Few things can tell us more about an artist than the type of followers he has found. Thanks to Count Reinhold Bethusy-Huc, who alone made this Homage to Kokoschka possible, we are not only enabled to see a large collection of the master's graphic work which he has brought together over the years with such unrivalled

1 *Saul and David: David hiding himself*. 1969. Lithograph. (71·13)

dedication, we are also allowed to understand what it was that inspired this devotion. The collector has overcome his reluctance and put down the history of his involvement with the artist and his oeuvre. In an age in which works of art are so frequently degraded into merchandise and collecting into a form of investment, this testimony is doubly valuable as proof that the concern of real art lovers is not with purpose, but with meaning. It is fitting, therefore, that this story of the growth of a unique collection should be preceded by the collector's own description of one of the master's late Biblical Illustrations, for it documents more tellingly than any historical appreciation what Kokoschka's creations mean to a man of our time:

> I am speaking about the lithograph *David hiding himself* from the sequence *Saul and David* 1969 (pl. 1).
>
> Night. The moon and the howling of dogs increase for me the feeling of man being utterly exposed in this world (a feeling we find so often in the poetry of Georg Trakl), a feeling of *Angst* or some fear aroused by the inexplicable. The lithograph is strictly auto-biographical as is every one of Kokoschka's creations; it is in fact a self-portrait. He creates an image here of his own great loneliness. It is an experience which has pervaded his whole life and which was essential to him. Without it he could not have said what he is going to bequeath to us. It is not for him a cause of suffering, he sought it, and from it alone he has drawn his great visionary works. Oskar Kokoschka, I believe, has been a lonely man through-out his life, however many people may have crowded around him. After every passionate commitment he hurled himself all the more vehemently into this loneliness, which has kept him isolated and has permitted him to give to the world with all the more prodigality.
>
> He leans on his staff, a shepherd's crook, a symbol of wandering, of leadership, of the elect, of a prophet. The movement of his left hand indicates that he will pull his cowl over his head so that no harm can befall him. He is no longer frightened by the Inexplicable. He knows about it now. Perhaps he is intent on letting us know too? He certainly wants us to open our eyes and see. He wants us to become fully human. For me his art is intensely religious.
>
> When Kokoschka depicts animals or flowers in water colours or drawings they bear the mark of this loneliness out of which they are created. Even a dead duck or a sinister toad are transformed by him into something mysteriously beautiful however ugly they may be on the surface, as sometimes with Rembrandt; they are infinitely moving as symbols of the inexplicable.

NOTES

1. *Mein Leben*, Munich, 1971; English translation *My Life*, London, 1974.
2. Printed in Oskar Kokoschka, *Schriften, 1907–1955*, ed. H. M. Wingler, Munich, 1956, pp. 337–41. There is an English translation in Edith Hoffmann, *Kokoschka*, London, 1947, pp. 285–87. The same book also contains many other utterances by Kokoschka.
3. *Mein Leben*, p. 184. The translation is my own.
4. Oskar Kokoschka, *Dramen und Bilder*, Leipzig, 1913.
5. *Mein Leben*, p. 72.
6. 'The Mask and the Face: The perception of physiognomic likeness in life and in art' in E. H. Gombrich, J. Hochberg and M. Black, *Art, Perception and Reality*, Baltimore, Maryland, 1972.
7. An extract is published under the title *Bewusstsein der Gesichte* in *Schriften* (as quoted above, note 2) pp. 342 f. The full text in Diether Schmidt, ed., *Schriften deutscher Künstler des zwanzigsten Jahrhunderts*, vol. I, Dresden, 1964, pp. 162–76.

The birth of a collection
Reinhold, Count Bethusy-Huc

When the Second World War came to an end on 8 May 1945 I was 15 years old. Even the remote little Bavarian town of Traunstein by the Chiemsee, where we lived, was engulfed by chaos. Hunger, bombed-out people, displaced persons, refugees, occupying troops. I had to go back to school, which I hated although it had undergone a 'colour change'. By great good fortune Dr Oskar Lang, art historian, painter, poet, composer and author of an important work on Anton Bruckner, who had been bombed out of his home in Munich, settled in our little town. He and his charming wife lived in one small room, where, to eke out a meagre existence, he would give talks on the old masters. These Saturday afternoons became my real school, and Lang became the decisive influence in my life. I vividly remember his first lectures, on Rembrandt and his Time, and still treasure two reproductions of Rembrandt etchings, the *Three Trees* and the *Annunciation to the Shepherds* he gave me. Not much later I met the Munich art dealer Günther Franke, a sensitive, unassuming and deeply religious art lover and connoisseur, who had taken enormous risks to save the works of so-called 'Degenerate Artists' during the Nazi period. Through him I made my first contact with modern art, including some of Oskar Kokoschka's works. I am deeply indebted to him for the unforgettable hours I spent with him and his circle of friends in his gallery at the Villa Stuck in Munich. It was Franke who introduced me to the pleasure of selecting from a welter of works of art being created all around us works that would endure. In these early impressionable years, my 'collecting' was, of necessity, restricted to reproductions. But at school I was put in charge of our show cases (no-one else wanted the task) and this gave me an early opportunity of observing people and their reactions to art.

My first major encounter with the works of Oskar Kokoschka was at the Retrospective Exhibition in the Haus der Kunst in Munich in the autumn of 1950. The experience was so over-powering that I spent an entire week in the presence of his pictures. I was then twenty years of age, and since that day Kokoschka's fascination for me has not changed.

A full year later, after a memorable performance of Berg's opera *Wozzek* in the Salzburg Festspielhaus, I was privileged to meet Oskar Kokoschka and his wife Olda face to face. His presence and his talk captivated me completely and bound me to him for life. As I sat in that little Austrian inn, a glass of local red wine before me on the table, my eyes were opened. I certainly learned more about life and people in that one evening than by the well-meaning efforts of all my teachers in many years of school. It is not possible to describe the unique quality of this meeting. This could only be experienced. If such happiness comes one's way once in one's lifetime, it behoves one to be thankful ever after. However, I might perhaps try to give an idea of the way he talked about his drawings for *The Concert* and how they came into being, for this is one of the most precious memories of this wonderful evening. In response to my saying how much I had been moved by their compassion and musical feeling, he literally recreated the drawings of the cycle before my eyes in talking about them. The expressions of his face vividly re-enacted the Variations of his model's expression as it changed from one drawing to the next to the strains of Beethoven's music and made me see those visions ultimately fulfilled in a tragic fate. When he had ended he fell silent. We parted and I walked for hours through the nocturnal streets of the beautiful city. The thoughts of what I had heard evoked in my mind much-loved verses by Georg Trakl, that great poet, who had been a friend of Kokoschka's and was as closely linked with Salzburg as Kokoschka himself.

In 1952 I met Kokoschka again in the city of Salzburg. In that year he wrote a dedication for me, the significance of which I did not grasp until much later:

'Für den lieben Jünger Reinhold Bethusy zur Erinnerung an OK 52'
(*To my dear disciple Reinhold Bethusy in memory of OK 52*)

In that year I acquired at the Welz gallery in Salzburg the portfolio *Variationen über ein Thema*, that is to say ten facsimiles of drawings for the 'Concert' which had stood at the beginning of our relationship, and the very rare first volume of *Kokoschka Handzeichnungen* edited by Dr Ernst Rathenau (Berlin, 1935). Kokoschka inscribed it for me with the following words:

'Eine Übersicht beendet kurz vor der Katastrophe, bereiten wir uns vor für eine kommende, doch bleiben wir stark im Sinn   O Kokoschka 1952'
(*a survey completed shortly before the catastrophe – let us be prepared for another to come, but let us remain stout-hearted*)

These two works formed the foundation stone of my collection.

From Salzburg I visited Venice for the first time. I wanted to see Kokoschka's *Prometheus Saga*, then on view at the Biennale. From that time onwards I have been following Kokoschka's steps – his world in pictures, *Orbis Pictus. His* visions of the *Salute* were for me as much unforgettable memories of Venice as my own visits to the Scuola di San Rocco or Tintoretto's tomb. In Florence I was determined to view the Duomo for the first time from the point from which Kokoschka had painted it. This quest has led me to discover a great deal of this wonderful city. It is a matter of much regret that, apart from the pastel drawings after Michelangelo's slaves in the *Florentiner Skizzenbuch*, little of his passionate devotion to Michelangelo, and of his illuminating interpretations of the man and his works found in his letters, has so far been published.

In 1953 I went to Hamburg to start my working life as a trainee in commerce. This was a difficult time for me. It was made bearable only by the kindness of a few wonderful people, among them Carl Georg Heise, the Director of the Hamburg Kunsthalle, and his charming wife. On my first visit to the Kunsthalle he offered to lend me a painting by Kokoschka, the *Armenviertel* (poor quarter) 'to decorate my room with', though he had never seen me before in his life. Another dear friend from these Hamburg days travelled with me to Salzburg, where we were privileged to see Kokoschka in his 'Schule des Sehens' on the terraces of Salzburg castle, and to listen to his inspiring talk at the Café Tomaselli.

In 1954 I left Germany for good, for no other reason than that I felt I did not belong. I went to England because I loved the country and her people. There I felt happy and free; in 1963 I became a Britsh citizen. How marvellous it was for me to be able to see Kokoschka in a concert hall, or visit him at his hotel, where I was allowed to admire one of his views of the river Thames he had just completed. In 1960 there was the memorable exhibition 'Kokoschka in England and Scotland' at Marlborough Fine Art Gallery to enjoy.

This was the time I started collecting posters, exhibition catalogues, books by and about Kokoschka, photographs and reproductions of his works. I tried to trace his steps and met numerous people who figured in his life, and saw many of the landscapes he had painted.

I met him again at the opening of his great retrospective exhibition at the Tate in 1962. This meant a great deal to him, as I was well aware.

Two years later, in 1965, I visited the Kokoschkas for the first time in their home in Villeneuve. I was greatly impressed by the simplicity with which he surrounded himself, and by the loveliness of his garden, full of irises and acquilegias (which I know so well from his water colours). In the background, *his* Lake Geneva, and *his* Dent du Midi.

In the following year, 1966, I travelled with my mother from Milan to Zurich to attend the opening of Kokoschka's great exhibition at the Kunsthaus. I had long wished fervently for a meeting between my mother and OK, and the fulfilment of this wish was a wonderful experience. It was immortalised for me by a most moving dedication he wrote for me on his *Pegasus* in 1968, the year of her death.

After my visit to Zurich I was at last in the position to contemplate buying some of his graphic works. It had been my wish from the first to acquire only works that had for me an intimate and personal significance. The first series I bought were his lithographs to his *Apulian Journey* and his *Homage to Hellas* (pl. 23).

I met Kokoschka again in London in 1967. He was then working on a large Thames landscape. To commemorate this meeting I bought his self-portrait of 1966 (pl. 12). I had been trying very hard in those days to persuade influential people that they should ask Kokoschka to draw lithographs of London. When his cycle *London from the River Thames* appeared, I was very happy.

In that same year I visited Prague for the first time. I met Dr Jan Tomeš, the author of the beautiful book *Kokoschka's Prague landscapes*, and his wife Helenka, who showed me the 'Golden City'. I visited the Villa Kramář, where a gardener still remembered Kokoschka painting the view, the tower from which he painted so many of his famous views of Prague, and the statue of Christ on Charles Bridge, which had become the inspiration for his intensely moving poster of Christmas 1945 (pl. 21). I also met Dr and Mrs K. B. Palkovský, the parents of his wife Olda, and they talked to me about OK. I began to see how important the years in Prague had been for Kokoschka, a fact which has perhaps not always been sufficiently stressed.

After a long and dismal winter, at the end of which I was deeply shaken by the sudden death of my beloved mother, I moved to Vienna. I found solace in a journey to Greece which opened a new world for me: new sights, and light such as I had never seen. There I encountered Kokoschka's *Mourning Woman* and his *Dionysos on a Donkey*. I went to Delphi to see the *Castilian Fountain* and to Aegina to admire the *Temple of Aphaia*. In Ithaca I lived through his *Odyssey*. His pictures became my pictures – it was all imbued with life, with tears and laughter. I meant to hold on to it all for ever, for myself and for others. That is why I collected.

On my return from Greece I visited Kokoschka's brother Bohuslav and his wife Minna and we became friends. Since he died unexpectedly at the age of 83 on 12 January, after I had penned these lines, I should like here to erect a modest monument to this man whom I regard as the last Romantic. It might bear the inscription: *Der ungehörte Ruf* (the Call nobody heard). I deeply mourn his passing; I learned much from him about Kokoschka the artist and Kokoschka the man. I also greatly liked his paintings, which were never finished, because he constantly changed them. I am glad to own some of his lithographs, watercolours and drawings as well as some of his literary works. I used to love to hear him read from his unpublished manuscripts. Among them is *Ein Vorfall* (an incident), published in 1916 in the Journal *Der Sturm* with three drawings by Oskar. There followed in 1920 *Adelina, oder der Abschied vom neunzehnten Lebensjahr* (Adelina, or the leavetaking from the nineteenth year of life; Kurt Wolff, Munich). He illustrated E. A. Rheinhardt's fairy tale *Der schöne Garten* (the fair garden) with four lithographs (1920, Strache, Vienna, Prague and Leipzig), and in 1926 he published *Geh, mach die Türe zu, es zieht* (close the door, will you, there is a draught), scenes from bourgeois life, with two etchings by Oskar. In 1947 Oskar drew eight illustrations to his brother's unpublished novel *Ketten in das Meer* (Chains into the Sea). It gives me great satisfaction that the work, later published under the title *Logbuch des B. K.* is available at one place at least complete with the reproductions of all Oskar's drawings and some photos. In one of his unfinished works *Urahne, Grossmutter, Mutter und OK* (Great grandmother, grandmother, mother and OK) Bohuslav wrote:

2 Illustration to *Ketten in das Meer* by Bohuslav Kokoschka. 1947. (46)

'Dem lieben Freund Reinhold Bethusy mit den herzlichsten Grüssen von seinem Bohuslav Kokoschka aus dem Liebhartstal Juli 1970'
(*To my dear friend Reinhold Bethusy with the very best wishes from Bohuslav Kokoschka, Liebhartstal July 1970*)

to which Oskar added:

'Bin mit meinem Bruder eine Seele und ein Leib, soll er lange leben! Oskar, Villeneuve, 28.X.70'
(*I am one with my brother in soul and body. May he live long! Oskar*)

I want to put on record this close relationship between Oskar and Bohuslav – a friendship like that of Tristan and Kurwenal, which I was privileged to witness many times. This unique relationship throws an important light on an essential trait in Oskar's character, and one of its most lovable aspects.

It was also in 1968 that I was fortunate to meet Hermine and Erich Kreuzer in Vienna, for it was they who enabled me to devote myself in a congenial atmosphere to my labours of love of documenting Kokoschka's life and work as fully as possible. One outcome of this activity was my collaboration with Dr Ernst Rathenau in the publication of the fourth volume of Kokoschka drawings, which was to me a great pleasure and privilege. What a unique opportunity to look through innumerable photos of drawings with Kokoschka, and assist in selecting those that were to go into the book. He would write on them in giant letters 'Ja, Ja, Ja' with exclamations marks, to make quite sure that Dr Rathenau would include them. On this occasion Kokoschka gave me a water colour *Eidechse und Heuschrecke* (Lizard and grasshopper). I saw at once that it represented a terrible drama, a typical Kokoschka drama. What he had made of those two animals was truly incredible! Equally remarkable was the way in which he changed this theme to transform it into a symbol of peace which was to serve as an introduction to his gigantic cycle of lithographs to the *Odyssey*. Kokoschka did not often make presents but when he did it was with an overwhelming generosity of the heart. It was the greatest joy for me that from time to time he adorned my prints or books with delightful inscriptions or drawings. I treasure these particularly as signs of his friendship and intimacy.

The year 1970 was an eventful one for me. In May of that year I acquired his *King Lear*; while he sat and signed each print, he paused a little to talk to me about it. These are unforgettable memories. I saw him again in Hamburg at the opening of his exhibition in the Museum für Kunst und Gewerbe, and there followed visits in autumn and at Christmas to his villa Delphin on Lake Geneva.

I now felt that my collection had reached such a size that I could think of a small exhibition. Mr Graham Reynolds and Sir John Pope-Hennessy of the Victoria and Albert Museum concurred with enthusiasm. What could be more appropriate than to make a loan of my small collection to this wonderful museum. It was the most suitable and most beautiful place in which to deposit what I held most dear. During the preparations for the exhibition in 1971 I was able to acquire the water colour *Fish on a Scottish Beach*, Karel Vogel's portrait of Kokoschka and Kokoschka's lithographs *Saul and David*.

It is a strange, almost uncanny experience to find oneself suddenly face to face with what one has experienced and collected through so many years. The light and atmosphere in the Bethnal Green Museum were exquisite and so were the people who helped to make this exhibition a memorable event. The beautiful massed chrysanthemums (flowers my mother had loved so much), the children who came to draw from the exhibits and once more, so many wonderful and charming people. What Gombrich had written in his introduction to the catalogue 'The collection is the outgrowth of love for a master who indeed inspires love' had become reality and had reached fulfilment through my loan to the Victoria and Albert Museum.

In recent years I have had the good fortune to acquire many beautiful graphic works of Kokoschka's: from the early post cards for the *Wiener Werkstätte*, the early ex libris, *die Jagd* in the programme for the cabaret *Die Fledermaus*, to his marvellous *Hiob*. In addition, more prints from the *Concert* series, *Maria Orska, Corona I, Max Reinhardt,* and *Lily Christiansen-Agoston,* all dating from the twenties. From the thirties there was *Trudl mit dem Strohhut* – which for me is like a Schubert song – and from recent years *Die Frösche* (pure Shakespearean visions these), his *Penthesilea,* the *Bal Masqué,* and *Longévité,* 1968. It gives me particular pleasure to possess the scores of Hindemith's *Mörder Hoffnung der Frauen,* Křenek's *Orpheus und Eurydike,* and Gottfried von Einem's *Träumende Knaben* (composed to Kokoschka's text), all inscribed for me by Kokoschka with delightful dedications. I am also most grateful to him for his lithograph *Amor und Psyche,* which means especially much to me because my father used to tell me the story. After burning much midnight oil I was able to acquire last year *Die Chinesische Mauer* and first editions of *Der Sturm* with portraits of Adolf Loos, Karl Kraus, Herwarth Walden, Yvette Guilbert and Blümner. By a happy circumstance I became the owner of Berta Patockova-Kokoschka's portrait of Oskar Kokoschka, a work which, like many others, I had tried for many years to acquire. Oskar Kokoschka, who completed the portrait jointly with his sister, considers it the only valid modelled portrait of himself, and he has said: 'This is what I shall look like when I am no longer alive'. All through his life Kokoschka was on very close terms with his sister. I also possess in my collection *Mein Lied,* a slim volume of selected poems of Berta's illustrated with seven drawings by Oskar. I made my last desperate fling for the *Women of Troy,* the biblical portrait of His Beatitude Benedictos I, Greek Orthodox Patriarch of Jerusalem, and finally the lithograph portrait of his mother dating from 1917.

In the summer of 1973 I visited the OKs in Villeneuve and showed them photos of my journey to Samothrace and Samos. Enthusiastic explanations interrupted his viewing: 'Look, my goats, my olive trees, my fishes!' I told him how I had climbed Mount Fengari with a shepherd and his dog, because according to legend Poseidon watched the battle of Troy from its top. The dog that walked by my side, following every step of mine, sometimes touching my body as if accidentally, and who bathed with me in a cool mountain stream and rested with us when we did, was clearly Kokoschka's *Shepherd's dog* as drawn by him at the Acropolis Museum (pl. 23). Kokoschka appeared to enjoy these tales. When I told him about flying fishes and dolphins he drew a dolphin for me. I was blissfully happy.

However, I did not merely collect the graphic works of Kokoschka. Throughout, I have always endeavoured to serve him and his work. Thus I have passed on to the Documentation Centre of Pöchlarn, the town where he was born, my reproductions of nearly 300 water colours and of his painted oeuvre, largely in colour, and all photographs of drawings not included in volumes 4 and 5 of Rathenau's *Kokoschka Drawings.*

I was able to assist Professor Friedrich Welz in the preparation of a catalogue of the graphic oeuvre, and I was privileged to collaborate with my dear friend Dr Ivan Fenyö in the publication of his enchanting work *Kokoschkas Frühe Graphik,* which enabled me to include one of his most remarkable paintings *Das Schweisstuch der Heiligen Veronika,* now in the Museum of Fine Arts, Budapest.

It gave me particular pleasure to assist Dr Ernst Rathenau in preparing for publication the fifth volume of *Kokoschka Handzeichnungen.*

At present I am engaged on a catalogue of all Kokoschka exhibitions (including exhibitions in which his works were well represented). I have already listed over 400 and I possess posters and catalogues of many of these.

I have also accumulated several hundred photographs relating to Kokoschka's life, pictures of his friends, sitters and models, etc. I was particularly anxious to find unpublished pictorial documents. To these I added letters to Carl Moll and others. In this way I hope to fill in the portrait of a painter who calls himself the last painter in the tradition of our Western culture.

Finally I should mention here the exhibition of Kokoschka's etchings and lithographs relating to Greece which was arranged by Dr Dimitrios Papastamos, Director of the National Pinakothek, in Athens earlier this year at the suggestion of Dr J. A. Sakellarakis of the National Archaeological Museum in Athens. My introduction to the catalogue, describing my journeys in Greece, was designed to be a humble offering to Oskar Kokoschka on the occasion of his 90th birthday, and at the same time my own 'Homage to Hellas' joined to his. He is my Vergil and I have to thank him for having opened my eyes.

I was privileged to revisit Oskar and Olda at Christmas 1975. There was brilliant winter sunshine on the Dent du Midi, late roses in the garden, a basket with apples and quince on the terrace, nearby a robin, and an occasional blackbird. Olda spoke of the bullfinches which destroyed the almond blossoms. At first, Kokoschka spoke of making a warning poster, but later he added, musingly: 'Perhaps the almond blossoms are there for the birds and not for us . . .'. When the sun set early in a Titian-red sky, Kokoschka picked up his pencil and drew at my request a shepherd with a crooked staff. For the first time I was allowed to watch. When he handed me the drawing I at once recognised in the shepherd a seer who, like Tiresias, comes down from the hills with his message and returns whence he came. At Kokoschka's request I then read him my account of my Greek journeys from the 'Homage to Hellas' exhibition catalogue. He constantly interrupted my reading with interested and interesting comments. It was an exciting, an unforgettable hour. Yet his appreciative words, his absolute and unshakeable confidence in me and his expressions of friendship when I took my leave, restored me to a wonderful sense of tranquillity.

In conclusion I should like to thank all those who have helped me to achieve this collection of graphic works by Kokoschka, and in particular to express my gratitude to the Victoria and Albert Museum and all my friends there who look after my collection with such touching and expert care, and who, by their enthusiasm, have found the means, despite these difficult times, to do homage to this great man and artist.

I should like to end with Kokoschka's own greeting: God bless you to and fro!

Nussdorf, January 1976

Translated by Lisbeth Gombrich

3 *Shepherd with a crooked staff*. 1975. Pencil.

The Symbolist legacy in the work of Kokoschka
Edith Hoffmann

The close connection between Kokoschka's work and certain traditions of European art is, at a time when most artists wish to establish their independence of the past, one of its most striking characteristics. Kokoschka has, in conversations with his various biographers as well as in his own writings, insisted on his indebtedness to certain Old Masters like Dürer, Brueghel and Maulpertsch, and H. M. Wingler has, in the introduction to his *Kokoschka – Das Werk des Malers*, added a few more names to this list. The fact that Kokoschka was also influenced by the generation which preceded his own has received less attention, although the connection between his earliest graphic style and the Jugendstil of Vienna has been noticed. But the young artist was exposed to yet another influence which was more profound than that of Art Nouveau. Recent publications and exhibitions have familiarised us with the phenomenon of European symbolism and the part it played, during the last 30 years of the 19th and the first decade of the 20th century, in cultural matters everywhere. Thus it has become clear that symbolism has, in the particular case of Kokoschka, contributed far more to his development than a few formal elements or the occasional motif: it has influenced his outlook on life and his conception of human relationships altogether, marked his literary style and supplied him with subject matter for his plays and pictures.

Symbolism reached Vienna a few years before Kokoschka began to take an interest in such matters and, when he became an art student, it was the modern movement of the day. Undoubtedly there was an element in his nature which responded to it, for he adopted many of the ideas of the symbolists immediately. Later he developed his own symbolism, which remained an important ingredient in his art even when his style changed and he became an expressionist. But, then, symbolism and expressionism are in any case closely related, as both movements were directed against naturalism and aimed at the subjective expression of those experiences which belong to the sphere of thoughts, emotions and dreams. Both were, of course, late phases of romanticism. As to Kokoschka, he remained an expressionist until about 1924, but even after that he never abandoned his very personal kind of symbolism.

We know that Kokoschka saw the work of the leading symbolist artists at the Kunstschau of 1909, where Gauguin, Munch, Toorop, Hodler and Minne were shown. In fact he must also have known some of it before. Hodler, for one, was famous in Vienna since the Secession had given him an exhibition in 1904. Minne's work had been on view in 1901, and his statue of a *Kneeling Boy* stood in the studio of the painter Carl Moll, who was one of the organisers of the Kunstschau and had included the statue in his *Self-portrait in my Studio* of 1906. L. Goldscheider records in his *Kokoschka* (1963) that the painter told him: 'Minne made a tremendous impression on me . . . it was from Minne that I took over a preference for these fleshless young Gothic bodies'. Other symbolist works were reproduced in the organ of the Secession, *Ver Sacrum*. Symbolism also found expression on the stage when plays by Strindberg, Maeterlinck or Wedekind were performed and, of course, in the literature of the day.

Kokoschka was naturally aware of this trend in the cultural life around him. The pessimistic fin-de-siècle attitude shared by most adherents of symbolism is reflected in his paintings of the period and has been commented upon in most discussions of his portraits. It remains to uncover the traces of symbolism in the subject matter of his plays and of his graphic work. Such an examination of the origins of his ideas and his iconography should reveal that symbolism reached far into our century and at the same time throw light on Kokoschka's very independent ways of using inherited material.

Two themes recur in Kokoschka's early plays as well as in his graphic work: the conflict between the sexes and the vulnerability of the artist. Both are central themes of symbolism. If the plays, as well as many of the paintings and drawings Kokoschka produced during the first years of his career, were inspired by personal experiences, as has always been maintained, it is certain that his sensibility had been sharpened by his acquaintance with certain symbolist works, and he had interpreted his experiences accordingly.

Kokoschka wrote his first text for the stage in 1907 and called it *Sphinx und Strohmann*.[1] The sphinx was, of course, one of the accepted symbols of the *femme fatale* and so frequent in 19th century literature and art from Heine to Franz von Stuck that it is unnecessary to speculate where Kokoschka had found it, although it is perhaps worth recalling that Kleist, in his play *Penthesilea*, which Kokoschka admired,[2] called his heroine a sphinx. Kokoschka's text was very fragmentary, but it managed to convey the opinion that love is ephemeral and woman, here ironically named 'Anima', a pernicious creature. She remains a mystery to the man who 'cannot see her' because she has turned his head on his shoulders. When Kokoschka, in 1917, wrote a new, fuller version of *Sphinx und Strohmann* which received the title *Hiob*, he made it clear that Anima was the biblical Eve who 'put the heavy cross on his shoulders'. In symbolism Eve was as frequent a symbol as was the sphinx.

Soon after *Sphinx und Strohmann* Kokoschka wrote another play, *Mörder Hoffnung der Frauen*, which was first staged at the Kunstschau of 1908.[3] This was a drama of love and death, enacted by characters described as 'Man' and 'Woman', who belong to an undefined antiquity. It was certainly inspired by Kleist's *Penthesilea*, a tragedy which equally represents love as a raging passion that leads to destruction. But, if there was a similarity of content and characterisation, Kokoschka had no use for the plot of a classical play which he replaced by a sequence of soliloquies and dialogues. The language used expressed in the most elementary fashion the close relation between love, lust and the thirst for blood. Such simple speech had not been used by German writers since Büchner had written his *Woyzeck* (1836), a play in which poetry and prose were similarly interwoven. Kokoschka has told us[4] that he used to read the works of Büchner, and it is no accident that the last scene of *Mörder Hoffnung der Frauen* is reminiscent of Woyzeck's murder of Marie. But, if such echoes can be discerned in Kokoschka's play, its main content owed more to certain writers closer to him in time. The most important of these was Strindberg, who had frequently dealt with the conflict between the 'new woman' and her male victim. The refusal to compromise with the hypocrisy of social conventions which he expressed in his writings appealed to Kokoschka as much as the free technique used in such plays as *Miss Julie*, where the traditional division into acts had been discarded. But his own plays were by no means mere imitations: his characters and the problems that moved them were detached from the realistic background against which Strindberg had set them, and, as they belonged to no particular period, they assumed the status of mythological figures.

The poster which Kokoschka designed for the performance of *Mörder Hoffnung der Frauen* sums up the play in a manner which could not fail to attract attention (pl. 4). Representing the flayed body of a dying or dead man with twisted limbs in the arms of a pale woman with brutal hands and bared teeth, it is a strange version of the Pietà as well as an evocation of that monster, the woman who kills through her love. The Mother of God and the 'woman' of the play have become one – a process which will appear less extraordinary if it is remembered that woman has often been described as personifying both the erotic and the maternal element. That the symbolist age was very conscious of this double aspect is best exemplified by Strindberg, whose Laura, in *The Father*, says to the Captain: 'Remember, it was as your second mother that I came into your

4 Poster. 1908. Lithograph.

5 Edvard Munch, *The Vampire*. 1895. Lithograph.

life. . . . The mother became the mistress – horrible. . . . The mother was your friend . . . but the woman was your enemy'.[5]

For Kokoschka it was perhaps natural to think of the Pietà when searching for a symbol of mournful love, for we know from many instances, that the tradition of religious art was never far from his mind. There is, however, a second image hidden behind his poster. A powerful influence he had inevitably absorbed was that of Munch, who was at the time much discussed in the German art world and whose graphic work was, in 1907, published in a book by Schiefler which every art student can be assumed to have seen. It is even possible that Strindberg's ideas had reached Kokoschka through the work of Munch, who had made them his own and invented many variations on the theme of the antagonism between the sexes. One of these, *The Vampire*, first executed as a painting in 1893 and repeated as a lithograph in 1895, shows a man hiding his face on the knees of a woman who bends over him lovingly and, at the same time, sucking blood from his neck (pl. 5). Comparison with Kokoschka's poster will show that the placing of both figures, the position of the woman's right arm and the long, open hair are the same, and so is the meaning of the group, even though Kokoschka's is more ambiguous.

The element of brutality apparent in the poster, which contrasts so strangely with the aesthetic appeal of its rhythmic contours and harmonious colours, is even more obvious in the four illustrations for *Mörder Hoffnung der Frauen*. Here the struggle for superiority is no longer a spiritual one, but physical and sadistic. Sadism too was part of the symbolist heritage. It had been an important factor in the writings of J.-K. Huysmans – Des Esseintes collected sadistic works of art – and the popularity of the famous Marquis had amused Beardsley, who put one of De Sade's books on Salome's dressing-table. In the work of the young Kokoschka sadism was frequent but never funny. He introduced the image of Phyllis – another *femme fatale* – riding on the back of Aristotle[7] in his illustrations for Albert Ehrenstein's *Tubutsch* (1911) and again in those for *Die Chinesische Mauer* by Karl Kraus (1914) because it was a familiar and unsurpassed symbol used by Hans Baldung, Lucas van Leyden and many others through the ages to express a perverse relationship which preoccupied him.

As Kokoschka matured his conceptions of human relations changed and he began to invent his own symbols. The picture of the *femme fatale* no longer satisfied him. It is true that in the series of lithographs for his play *Der Gefesselte Kolumbus* (1913) he still represented his heroine as Eve with the apple. In *Oh Ewigkeit, Du Donnerwort* (*Bachkantate*, 1914), however, the woman has become a symbol of life. Man and woman are carried through the storm together in the painting *The Tempest* (1914), and her head rests peacefully on his shoulder. This is a composition invented by Max Klinger, a symbolist artist much admired by Klimt and Munch: he had etched a plate for his album *Ein Leben* (1884) in which a couple, reminiscent of Kokoschka's lovers, rested in a shell and this was surrounded by space like Kokoschka's boat by water.

The belief in the complex relationship between the sexes and the mingling of biblical themes with contemporary ideas which Kokoschka had taken over from the symbolists and which can be found in the Pietà poster even played a part in the self-portrait which he designed in 1909, to be used in a poster for the magazine *Der Sturm* in 1910 and then again for a lecture he gave in 1912.[8] One of the striking features of this dramatic image is the gesture of the left hand, which points to a wound on the right side of the bare chest. It is impossible to see it and not to think of the wound the crucified Christ received from the lance of the Roman soldier.[9] To identify himself thus with Christ was bold on the part of the artist, but not entirely new. Before the 19th century it seems to have occurred only once: in Dürer's *Self-portrait* of 1500 where it had a different meaning. In the 19th century Gauguin was probably the first well-known painter who associated the misunderstood and suffering artist with Christ when he painted himself 'on the Mount of Olives' (1889). The theme was developed by Ensor whose *Self-portrait in Hell*, accompanied by the cock of St Peter, appeared in 1898 on the cover of *La Plume* and may thus have been known to Munch, who also painted himself 'In Hell' in the same year.[10] He also made a woodcut (1898) known as *Allegory – The flower of Pain* which was not exactly a self-portrait but shows a youth holding his hand to a chest wound from which blood flows, giving life to a flower – 'the flower of art which is fed by the artist's heart blood'[11] – and this is closely related to Kokoschka, in whose self-portrait the wound is of primary importance. One might even say that he was obsessed by the image of the wound, which is also mentioned in *Mörder Hoffnung der Frauen* – but there it is inflicted by the woman on the man. This gives a special meaning to all the self-portraits in which Kokoschka shows himself pointing to himself or his wound and closes the iconographic circle: like Munch's young man in the painting *Separation* (1894) who holds a bleeding hand to his chest,[12] he suffered through love more than through the isolation and persecution to which Gauguin and Ensor had referred.

Kokoschka repeated the gesture of the pointing hand, which is, by the way, here much like that of Dürer in his *Self-portrait* of 1500, in his self-portraits of 1913 and 1917, but the wound had disappeared, and one is thus more reminded of an *Ecce homo* representation. That Kokoschka was still identifying himself with Christ is finally proved by his painting *Knight Errant* (1915), in which he showed himself prostrate on the ground, under a sky on which the letters 'ES' recall the dying Christ's 'Eli, lama sabachthani – My God, why hast thou forsaken me?' The small sphinx in the background, on the other hand, indicates that he was at the same time still considering the other sex as one of the causes of human suffering.

However, some time later Kokoschka made a drawing of *The Agony in the Garden* (pl. 10; 1916), and now all symbolic implications had disappeared, although Christ still had the features of Kokoschka. This drawing is just an illustration of the New Testament, like all the lithographs belonging to the series *Die Passion*, for which it was a preparatory sketch. The *Knight Errant* had been the last example of Kokoschka's indebtedness to the symbolist movement.

NOTES

1. *Oskar Kokoschka – Schriften, 1907–1955*, ed. H. M. Wingler, Munich, 1956, pp. 153–67.
2. Edith Hoffmann: *Kokoschka – Life and Work*, London, 1947, p. 33.
3. Wingler: op. cit., p. 455, suggests that the play could have been performed in 1908 or 1909. In H. M. Wingler and F. Welz, *O. Kokoschka – Das druckgraphische Werk*, Salzburg, 1975, No. 31, where the poster made for the performance is discussed, the date of the first night is given as 4 July 1909.
4. Edith Hoffmann: op. cit., p. 33.
5. Quoted from *Six Plays of Strindberg*, translated by E. Sprigge, Doubleday, Anchor Books, 1955.
6. J. P. Hodin, in *Oskar Kokoschka – The Artist and his Time*, London, 1966, p. 87, has commented on their 'common ambivalent attitude towards women'.
7. See also W. Hofmann, *Nana – Mythos und Wirklichkeit*, Cologne, 1973, p. 174.
8. H. M. Wingler and F. Welz, *O. Kokoschka – Das druckgraphische Werk*, Salzburg, 1975, Nos. 32 and 33.
9. G. Svenaeus, *Edvard Munch – Das Universum der Melancholie*, Lund, 1968, traces the open chest wound to pietistic iconography.
10. G. Svenaeus, op. cit., p. 120, seems to suggest that Munch's painting was inspired by Rimbaud's *Une saison en enfer*.
11. See J. A. Schmoll gen. Eisenwerth, 'Munch und Rodin' in *E. Munch: Probleme – Forschungen – Thesen*, ed. H. Bock and G. Busch, Munich, 1973, p. 104.
12. G. Svenaeus, op. cit., p. 168.

On Oskar Kokoschka's portrait of Yvette Guilbert
Fritz Novotny

This picture of Yvette Guilbert (pl. 6) is one of twelve portraits of well known contemporaries[1] whom Oskar Kokoschka drew in the years between 1910–1916. The portraits were published in rapid succession in the magazine *Der Sturm* under the title *Menschenköpfe* (Portraits). Kokoschka's technique underwent some changes during this period and his approach varied with the personality of the sitter but the pure line dictated by the reproductive process gave this loosely connected series a certain cohesion.

These portraits represent Kokoschka's first great achievement both in his development of the art of portraiture and in his mastery of drawing. That of Yvette Guilbert is no exception and, being one of the earliest in the series, it is an early example of Expressionism.

The term 'Expressionism' demands a more detailed explanation. Its meaning is brought out by a comparison between Kokoschka's portrait of Yvette Guilbert and a lithographic portrait of the celebrated diseuse[2] (pl. 7) drawn by Toulouse-Lautrec seventeen years earlier. Both portraits show a profile of her head and neck turned to the right but the differences in their treatment provide an insight into the deep change in artistic concepts and presentation that took place around the turn of the century. Toulouse-Lautrec's drawing is a work of late Impressionism. Light is suggested by the economical use of delicate shadows in the face and scarcely perceptible curves to the contours of the profile merge it with the total emptiness of the white space surrounding it. The background is seen instinctively, barely consciously, as the glare of the footlights. But should the inky blob of the bow tie under the neck be considered as contributing to this vaguely impressionistic view of corporeality, lighting and atmosphere?

By contrast, at first glance, everything seems radically different in Kokoschka's drawing with its structure of needlesharp lines in the face and wild strokes in the hair. In this drawing, as well, everything is highlighted by the total blankness of the white background, but the face is not modelled in the round. The delicate shadings do not contribute to its plasticity as is the case in Toulouse-Lautrec's portrait, but drawn along, and in some cases, outside the contours of the neck and forehead, project the head out of the surrounding blankness of the background. Various indeterminate shadings in their hair give the same effect. Nor does Kokoschka try and give an illusion of light. An open shape of a living, vibrating sketch predominates, representing a fundamental change in the relationship between the background and the drawn lines.

Finally, while thus enumerating the differences between these two portraits, the difference in drawing technique should be remarked upon. The jagged, barbed lines of Kokoschka contrast with the unbroken flowing contours of Toulouse-Lautrec and as a result of their intrinsic qualities give a different illustrative content to the two portraits. Compare the hardness and sharpness of the face of the ageing woman as she sings a serious chanson in the portrait by Kokoschka with Toulouse-Lautrec's gentle line, which just as effectively captures the striking ugliness of the youthful face. In spite of the apparent simplicity of method, almost bordering on caricature, Toulouse-Lautrec's portrait is a more cunning commentary on the sitter – it is the fin-de-siècle mode of expression.

Considering the two drawings even more closely, it is apparent that in Toulouse-Lautrec's the blankness not only gives an effect of light but also has something in common with Kokoschka's. The strong accentuation of the black bow tie demonstrates this similarity between the two artists although at a cursory glance their methods of drawing seem so contrasting. The essential characteristic of Early Expressionism is the emergence of the open form created in Kokoschka's work by the varying intensity of the shading. This breakthrough was remarkably more radical in some other of

6 *Yvette Guilbert.* 1911. Line-block. (15)

7 *Yvette Guilbert* by H. de Toulouse-Lautrec. 1893. Lithograph from the series *Le Café-Concert*.

Kokoschka's drawings of the same period, such as those for Ehrenstein's *Tubutsch* or for his own drama *Mörder Hoffnung der Frauen* (Murderer Hope of Women). These examples differ from the series of portraits for *Der Sturm* because, instead of reproducing in a concentrated form something he saw before him, the artist composed with shapes and scenes from his own imagination. Above all they show the mysterious connection between the blank background and the drawn lines while in the *Sturm* drawings there is no connection between the blank surface of the picture and the excessive graphic shapes made up of ghostly wild strokes. That extreme form of artistic expression lasted only a short time in Kokoschka's graphic oeuvre. Since then this mysterious relationship between the blank surface and the structure of the drawing has been visible in varying degrees.

In making such a comparison, it must not be overlooked that Toulouse-Lautrec's oeuvre also includes intensive forms of drawing, with many a similarity to Kokoschka's graphic style in the portrait of Yvette Guilbert. They crop up only on occasion but are clearly defined. The lithograph of the *Menu Hébrard*, which appeared the year after Guilbert's portrait, has a biting sharpness of line and no illusionist effect associated with Impressionism. The impressionist effects, on the other hand, remain present in his art in varying degrees. In the later series of Yvette Guilbert on the stage, done in 1898 and known as the *Série Anglaise*, it is even an Impressionism of exceptional artistic fineness and inspired graphic skill. Thus the work of both these artists provides a continuous highly varied find of riches.

It is worth drawing attention to the part played by the background of a picture and the artist's attitude to it. It plays a part as soon as the artist begins to create, whether he is aware of it or not. Before the first stroke is made on the paper it is often felt by him as a mysterious demanding power, not simply as something to be taken for granted. Space is a fundamental element, of course, in all painting and drawing but it is given greater emphasis in the latter. In 'realistic' painting, using the term in its widest sense, the elementary irrefutable power of the background appears in countless variants until it reaches an extreme with Impressionism. Impressionist pictures achieved with their picturesque small scale a maximum radical fusion of the surface and the illusion of space: the 'Doppelgesicht' of this painting, in which the surface is much more than a mere neutral screen on which to project the illusion. This last and most extreme stage of Impressionism was the fundamental basis for the art of both Toulouse-Lautrec and Kokoschka, in spite of all their apparent differences.

In the work of these two great draughtsmen the connection between the surfaces and the graphic structures is evident in one of its most distinctive forms and contributes to the effectiveness of their drawings as interpretations of the moving, inner and outer world, as well as of its general organic construction. Naturally this is valid to a certain degree for all drawings depicting visible objects, but the extent to which it is true varies with the realistic intensity of the content. At the time Toulouse-Lautrec was working, the revolutionary power of Cézanne's drawings made this overwhelmingly evident. It was part of a new role played by the surface in giving the illusion of space and body and ultimately led to the rejection of the portrayal of 'reality' in painting. This radical relationship between the surface and the drawn lines in an art which turned away from illustration is not relevant to the theme of this short discussion.

In conclusion it should be mentioned that in their portraits both Kokoschka and Toulouse-Lautrec used the power of the picture surface to contribute to the personality of their sitters. The only difference in this respect between them is that what emerges in Kokoschka as the achievement of a single individual is, in Toulouse-Lautrec's case, part of the general basic attitude of a whole era embedded in Late Impressionism. That his art was leading on to something new is shown by the role his work played in the development of the poster with its 'meaningful blanks'. But in this aspect of his work he was a good way removed from Impressionism, which was not concerned with Toulouse-Lautrec's principal interest: the theme of Man. Like Kokoschka he was one of the greatest portrayers of people of his time. Their talent for drawing people provides an undeniable connection between the two artists, however dissimilar they may appear as a whole. They also have in common a hidden method of fusing the picture's surface with the artistic form.

NOTES

1. For the identities of the other sitters see note 1 to *Der Sturm*.
2. From the series *Le Café-Concert*, 1893, to which Toulouse-Lautrec contributed 11 lithographs.

*Der Sturm**
Hans Bolliger

On 3 March 1910, in Berlin–Halensee, the first edition of the magazine *Der Sturm* (The Storm) appeared. It was a weekly journal of culture and the arts, and the publisher was Herwarth Walden.

The first numbers were the size of a newspaper, arranged in three columns and printed on newspaper in an edition numbering 30,000. There were about eight pages and the price was originally 10 pfennigs. From March 1913 until 1916 the magazine appeared every fortnight; from 1917—1923 every month; in 1924 every quarter and from 1925—1929 it once more appeared monthly. From 1930 until it finally closed down in 1932, it appeared only irregularly. In 1919 it appeared printed in a smaller folio size, but the range was greater.

When Herwarth Walden began to publish *Der Sturm* he was not an unknown figure. Born on 18 September 1878 in Berlin, the son of a Jewish doctor, he studied at the Berlin Conservatory and was awarded the Liszt Scholarship for his distinguished piano playing. This took him to Italy for a two year stay. He became a music critic, composer, literary figure and editor of short-lived literary magazines such as *Der Morgen* (Morning), *Der Komet* (Comet), *Der Neue Weg* (the New Way). He was married for some years to Else Lasker-Schüler, the writer.

Accompanying the first number of *Der Sturm* was the explanation: 'This is the fourth time we have published a new magazine. On three occasions, people have tried to hinder us by inconsiderately breaking contracts – our activities were considered by too many people as a thorn in the flesh. We have, therefore, decided to be our own publishers, for we are glad that culture and the arts can still be offered to the public instead of journalism and shoddy magazines.'

In number 12 of the first year's edition Walden published a full page drawing of the writer Karl Kraus, done by a young Austrian artist Oskar Kokoschka, who had followed up an invitation from Walden, only too glad to be able to exchange the unsympathetic atmosphere of his native country for the stimulating avant-garde atmosphere of Berlin. This drawing was the first in Kokoschka's series of luxuriantly expressive portraits of contemporaries[1] which appeared under the title *Menschenköpfe* (Human heads) at irregular intervals in *Der Sturm*. Blümner, Dehmel, Yvette Guilbert, Kerr, Adolf Loos, Paul Scheerbart, Herwarth and Nell Walden among others were sitters. A number of his strangely tense drawings like *Sphinx und Strohmann* (The Sphinx and the Straw Man) and *Flucht aus dem Paradies* (Flight from Paradise) were also published.

The literary content of the first editions was provided by the young writers and literary figures of the disintegrating Berlin Expressionism like the actor Rudolf Blümner, the poet Albert Ehrenstein and Kokoschka,[2] with valuable contributions from writers of the older generation such as the poets Peter Altenberg, Peter Hille and Arno Holz, Karl Kraus, publisher of *Die Fackel* (The Torch), the architect Adolf Loos and Strindberg.[3]

In the very same year Walden defended the radical artists of the New Secession, 'The Berlin Secessions Rejects', showing their dramatic paintings in the 'Macht' Gallery. In 1911, the artists belonging to 'Die Brücke' joined forces with *Der Sturm* after moving to Berlin. Till January of the following year they published almost weekly drawings of original woodcuts. Heckel, Kirchner, Pechstein, Schmidt-Rottluff, and even Emil Nolde, a former member of 'Die Brücke' contributed countless drawings. Their favourite media were original woodcuts, linocuts and lithographs, which were particularly effective on the coarse grained newspaper with the clean black and white contrast and also eliminated the cost of expensive typesetting. As well as works by Kokoschka and the artists of 'Die Brücke', the magazine *Der Sturm* offered woodcuts, lithographs and reproductions by a wide variety of other avant-garde artists.[4]

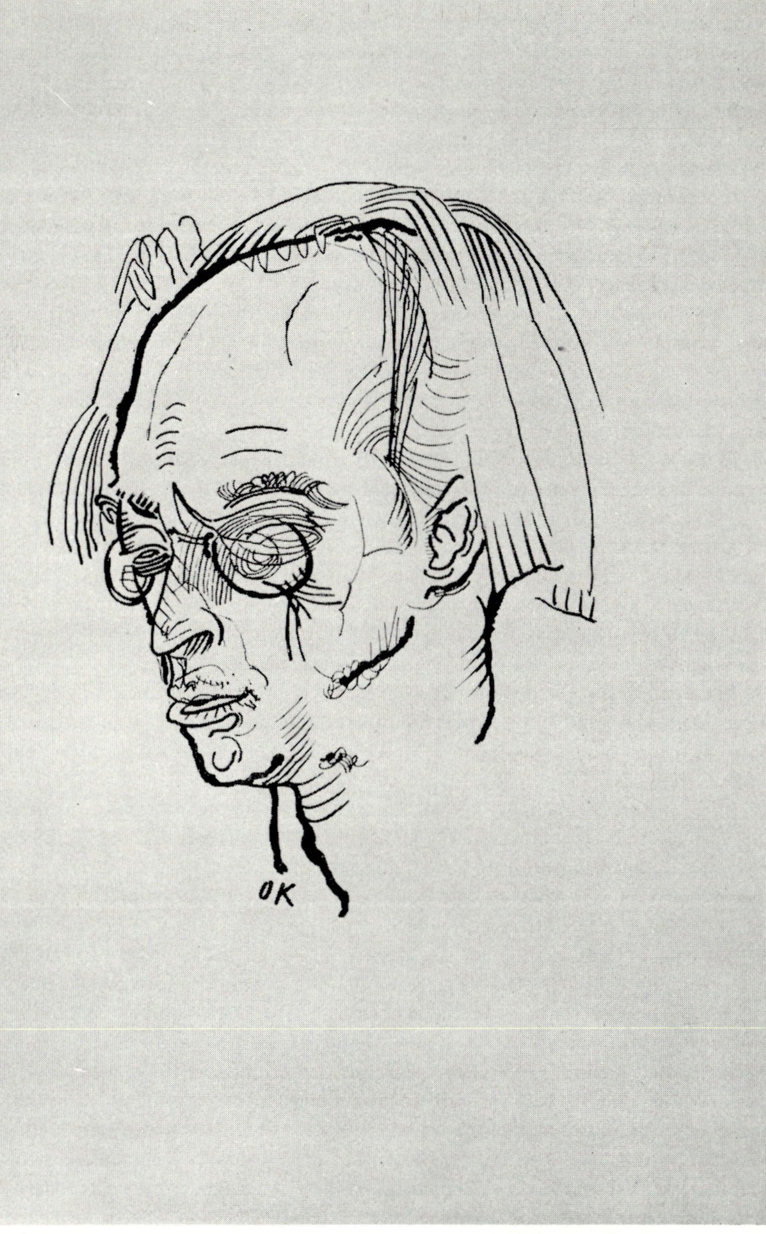

8 *Herwarth Walden.* 1910. Line-block. (15)

In 1912 the magazine was already such a going concern that they were able to move into new premises at 18 Potsdam Street. Nell Roslund-Walden, the musician, painter and writer, was the person who both stimulated Walden and fought by his side, and for 14 years she shared in the decision-making about the course and development of the *Sturm* and she took upon herself the heavy burden of the administrative side of the magazine.

It soon became clear that young artists needed, above all, places to display their works, and so in March 1912 the 'Sturm' gallery was affiliated to the magazine and the gallery was opened with an exhibition by the 'Blaue Reiter' group and a special exhibition of Kokoschka's works.

In February 1912 the Italian Futurists had an exhibition in the Bernheim Gallery in Paris. Walden contacted them and in April opened the first Futurist exhibition in Germany at 34 Tiergarten Street. The exhibition was a spectacular event and an overwhelming success and on many days attracted more than 1,000 visitors.

At the same time new members of different nationalities joined the team of workers. From every corner of Europe the new revolutionary, fermenting artistic powers were tracked down and brought together, and contacts made between both Italy and France. Soon the 'Sturm' and its 'Tribune Gallery' were the centres for all the artists who were seeking a new form of visual or literary expression.

In the *Sturm* the Futurists published their manifesto and advertised their movement with both literature and art. It contained as yet unpublished selections from Kandinsky's highly influential article 'On the Spiritual in Art', and several chapters from the book *Der Blaue Reiter* by D. Burljuk and August Macke. Guillaume Appolinaire, the intellectual leader of French modern painters, gave a lecture in the 'Sturm' Gallery on 'The beginning of Cubism' and published the texts of 'Réalité peinture pure' and 'Modern Painting', and 'Zone' among others. The controversial article 'On Light' by Robert Delaunay appeared, translated by Paul Klee; and from Leger the contribution 'The origins of contemporary painting and its representational value'.

In the gallery there were exhibitions of French graphic works, and paintings by Braque, Derain, Friesz, Laurencin and Picasso. There followed exhibitions by Ensor, Kandinsky, Delaunay, Klee, Marc, Severini, Archipenko, Macke, Jawlensky, Chagall, Gleizes, Metzinger, Duchamp-Villon, and Jacques Villon.

There was feverish activity in 'Der Sturm'. With stunning intuitive sense, Walden picked up everywhere everything that was new, avant-garde and significant, and discovered the leaders of it, organised lectures and wrote theoretical and polemical articles for *Der Sturm*. He travelled tirelessly, looking for new places to hold exhibitions as well as for new talent, constantly engrossed in texts, involved in heated discussions which broke out in the gallery, in the publisher's office or in the 'Rotonde' in Paris, in the 'Café des Westens' in Berlin, and in the very artists' studios.

In Autumn 1913 thanks to the generous financial support of Bernhard Koehler, the Berlin art collector and patron, Walden was able to hold the first German Autumn Exhibition with 366 works by over 80 artists from America, Germany, France, Italy, Russia, Switzerland and Spain. The list of contributors[5] alone is proof of the organiser's unerring instinct for talent and of his boldness. The show was vital for Walden's artistic programme. In the 'Sturm' all the artists were to allow themselves to be guided by their native backgrounds. They were to represent things 'according to their own personal experiences', 'to paint what they saw with their innermost beings'. Thus it becomes clear that Walden saw 'Expressionism' as a collective term for all modern artistic movements – Futurism, Expressionism in the sense of 'Die Brücke' and 'Der Blaue Reiter' and Cubism.

In a polemical article entitled 'Nachrichtung', Walden fought back with dialectic sharpness and biting irony against the criticisms of the press which were published in an *Encyclopedia of German Art Criticism* composed of newspaper reports about the autumn collection. The following are some of the choicest criticisms:

9 *Karl Kraus.* 1910. Line-block. (15)

'Disgusting to the public; Charlatans; impertinent theorisers; garish oafs; Hottentots in shirts; a horde of paint splashing monkeys; crazed daubs; neurotic colourists; topsy turvy ideas; madness in all its extremes; coconut shies for the village fair (Robert Delaunay) – thickly painted blobs of bad colour; a witches' sabbath; clownish somersaults; niggers in a top hat; infants in evening dress; the newest artistic disease; mongrel talents; philistines; madness of the sane; mad creations of the imagination; fashions with no chance of development; madness in paint; showing off; a lunatic's picture gallery; sensation seeking aesthetic decadents'.

In 1914 the scope of 'Der Sturm' was extended to include travelling exhibitions which visited towns all over Europe and even went to Tokyo, and it also founded its own publishing house. The 'Sturm' poets, such as Peter Baum, Hermann Essig, Runge, Schreyer and Kurt Schwitters, appeared in print. The poems of Herwarth Walden and Kokoschka's drama *Mörder Hoffnung der Frauen* (Murderer Hope of Women) were also published. The sculptor, Archipenko and the painters Chagall, Heemskerck, Klee and Schwitters were first recognised in the *Sturm*. Blümner and Gleizes wrote studies on Cubism, and the influential books by Walden, *Expressionism, the turning point in Art, Insight into Art* and *The New Painting*, were also published.

In 1917, the 'Sturm' bookshop was opened in 138a Potsdam Street, where the 'Sturm' publications and influential writings on modern literature and art were circulated.

In 1918, a 'Sturm' art school and theatre were founded, and in the *Diaries of the Sturm Stage* the theories of 'Der Sturm' towards a new theatre culture were laid down. At about the same time, the public was allowed in to see Walden's private art collection a unique cross-section of representative works by the artists.

Even during the war the exhibitions were continued and included works by the 'enemy', namely by the Russians Chagall, Archipenko and Kandinsky. The *Sturm* took no sides in the war, nor did it publish propaganda, as Franz Pfemfert in his *Aktion* also avoided doing. Of course there were almost monthly reports of the bloody toll which the war took of young painters' and poets' lives. First the artists August Macke, Boccioni and Franz Marc, then the poet Hermann Essig were killed. Shortly afterwards the lyric writer August Stramm fell in action – he was Walden's greatest discovery and it is to his eternal credit that he gave Stramm his fullest support at a time when the despairing writer was being rejected by other literary circles. During the war, the team of writers dwindled to only a small group which, passionately supporting Stramm's work, created a new form of poetry which has gone down in history as being representative of what the 'Sturm' really stands for. Through intensive study Blümner, Schreyer and Walden laid down new theories of poetic form under the name of 'Verbal Art'. At hundreds of 'Sturm' evenings in Berlin and throughout Germany the talented actor and reciter Blümner read out the poems of August Stramm. After the war important new contributors such as Hans Arp, Kurt Schwitters, Rudolf Bauer, Willi Baumeister, Molzahn, Otto Nebel and Oskar Schlemmer joined the magazine.

In September 1921 they were able to put on the 100th exhibition. In 1922 the French Dadaists[6] and the new generation of Italian writers also joined forces with 'Der Sturm'. In 1924, Herwarth and Nell Walden separated, and 'Der Sturm' gradually began to fade out. Although Walden continued to hold exhibitions and the magazine still appeared, the old impact was no longer there, and somehow the earlier sure instinct for what was relevant and forward-looking had disappeared.

On 28 September 1928, in honour of his 50th birthday, a Herwarth Walden Evening was held in the 'Theater am Schiffbauerdamm' in Berlin, and a special edition of *Der Sturm* was published.

An honorary committee, including the architects Peter Behrens and Erich Mendelsohn, the painters E. L. Kirchner, Moholy-Nagy and Schlemmer, the futurist Marinetti, and the choreographer Rudolf Laban formulated this appeal:

'We hope that both public and private art circles will help to make it possible for Herwarth Walden's intellectual and artistic powers to continue to flourish both within "Der Sturm" and outside it.' The appeal was signed by 340 artists of all nationalities but how many artists, how many of his old friends' names were missing. The appeal remained a purely rhetorical one. And there was nobody who did not feel how abandoned Walden had become.

In 1932 Walden went to Russia. From 1938–39 we hear his voice a few times in the magazine *Das Wort* (The Word) for German emigrés in Moscow. There are small 'notes made in the margin', brief polemical observations on cultural and literary events during the Third Reich. Once he had the opportunity, in an article called 'Vulgar Expressionism' to take part in a 'Discussion on Expressionism' in which he defended them against reproaches and accusations of being the forerunners of Fascism (*Das Wort*, 1938, Edition 2). Then nothing more is heard or seen of him. Today, now that information about Walden is missing and that Nell Walden's famous collection has been broken up,[7] we retain only the memory of a fascinatingly varied personality, highly gifted intellectually, and with a true pioneer spirit. Even though his taste may have faltered in his later years, and even though so much of what appeared in *Der Sturm* has found no lasting fame with subsequent generations, what he did in the name of new art and on behalf of many artists who are now known throughout the world is immeasurable.

But in *Der Sturm* this richest, most varied and comprehensive document on the Avant-garde in art he has left behind an everlasting memorial. There was no magazine published in the vital years between 1910 and 1932 in which the then current ideas and movements in art were so fully and so authentically documented.[8]

NOTES

* A revised version of the introduction to the exhibition catalogue *Der Sturm*, Kunstgewerbe Museum, Zurich, 1955

1. The sitters for this series were Rudolf Blümner, Richard Dehmel, Gertrud Eysoldt, Yvette Guilbert, Alfred Kerr, Karl Kraus, Mechthild Lichnowsky, Adolf Loos, Paul Scheerbart, Herwarth Walden, Nell Walden and Claire Waldorf.
2. Other contributors with these sympathies included Alfred Doblin, Jacob von Hoddis, Else Lasker-Schü¹er, Alfred Liechtenstein, René Schickelé and Paul Zech.
3. The following were also to be found amongst the contributors: Hermann Bang, Heinrich Mann, Alfred Mombert, Paul Scheerbart, Frank Wedekind, Eduard Bernstein, Lujo Brentano, August Forel and Sigmund Freud.
4. These included: Archipenko, Arp, Balla, Baumeister, Boccioni, Brancusi, Campendonk, Chagall, Delaunay, Max Ernst, Feininger, Filla, Gleizes, Gris, Hartley, Heemskerck, Hodler, Itten, Janco, Jawlensky, Kadar, Kandinsky, Kiesler, Klee, Kubin, Larionov, Laurencin, Léger, Lüthy, Macke, Malevitsch, Marc, Marcoussis, Meidner, Metzinger, Moholy-Nagy, Molzahn, Moilliet, Mondrian, Mucha, Münter, Munch, Nebel, Pascin, Picabia, Picasso, Prampolini, Man Ray, von Rebay, O. Van Rees, Hans Richter, Russolo, Schelfhout, Schlemmer, Schreyer, Schrimpf, Schwitters, Seehaus, Segal, Servranckx, Severini, Sluyters, Soffici, Topp, Uhden, Vordemberge-Gildewart, Nell Walden, Wauer, von Werefkin.
5. These included: Archipenko, Arp, Balla, Boccioni, Burljuk, Campendonk, Carra, Chagall, Robert and Sonja Delaunay, Max Ernst, Feininger, Gleizes, Hermann Huber, Jawlensky, Kandinsky, Klee, Kokoschka, Larionov, Léger, Macke, Marc, Marcoussis, Metzinger, Moilliet, Mondrian, Picabia, Russolo, Severini, von Werefkin and a small special showing of works by Henri Rousseau.
6. Including Aragon, Breton, Eluard, Fraenkel, Péret, Ribemont-Dessaignes, Soupault and Tristan Tzara.
7. Auctioned 24/25 November 1954 at the 20th Auction of the Stuttgarter Kunstkabinett.
8. A richly documented book in memory of Herwarth Walden was put together by Nell Walden, Lothar Schreyer and Otto Nebel: *Der Sturm*, Woldemar Klein, 1954.

Kokoschka's 'Agony in the Garden'
Jan Tomeš

In the New Testament in the words of Matthew we hear of Christ's great moments of indecision, the dreadful doubts which were present in his mind in the ancient olive groves with Judea in the background. We hear of his wavering hesitation, which is incorporated in one of the deepest symbols of the scriptures '. . . and he went a little farther and fell on his face and prayed, saying, O my Father, if it be possible, let this cup pass from me . . .'(26, 39). Luke also says '. . . and there appeared an angel unto him from heaven, strengthening him . . . '(22, 43).

For artists of the Middle Ages, the Gothic era and even the Early Renaissance, this theme was a familiar part of their own inner world, an undisputed refuge for a Christian philosophy of life, the unique parable of life, deeds and things. We meet Christ in conversation with his Father in a whole line of cycles of the Passion which were painted by anonymous and famous artists alike; in the kiss of Judas which Giotto painted in the Scrovegni Chapel in Padua in 1305; in one of the altar pictures still in existence painted by the Master of Třeboň (Wittingau); and in the cycle by Albrecht Altdorfer (1518).

What can be a 20th century artists's motive, however, in tackling such a theme, when it is not merely a commission done by a more or less skilled craftsman but a fantastically violent personal inner experience?

In 1963 Oskar Kokoschka had the opportunity in London to talk about his drawings. In this text, which is certainly one of the artist's most significant testimonies on his own work, his concepts and his relationship to other artists, there are some passing remarks about the personality of Albrecht Dürer – the creator of the Great Passion – and about Albrecht Altdorfer, who made an exceptional comment on the sufferings of Christ. Oskar Kokoschka actually said: 'I love Dürer because of his connection with the Danube School. Their landscape is the landscape of my childhood and adolescence. The story of St. Florian in the work of Altdorfer has this same background. If I had the courage, I would attempt the Passion. I am attracted to the idea of acknowledging the existence of God . . .' and adds: 'I would not do it with great iconographic exactitude. For that I am not Christian enough in the religious sense . . .'

It is strange that Oskar Kokoschka did not say at that time 'I should attempt the Passion *once more*', for he could scarcely have forgotten the cycle of six lithographs with which he had struggled as early as 1916, when he was thirty. In these he portrayed the sufferings of Man. Today, however, we sense the uncertainty of the master when confronted with the complex, hidden depths of the Biblical material. The creator of the immortal 'Singer of Kyme' (Ulysses) and Shakespeare's tragedies (*King Lear*) is unsure of himself. The incomplete Kokoschka cycle of the Passion published by Cassirer was accompanied by a series of drawings which included one of exceptional symbolism and incredible artistic merit, namely *The Agony in the Garden* (pl. 10).[1] This drawing took as its theme the quoted text of the Gospels and had as its content the symbol of sacrifice wittingly undertaken. What drove him to do this work were, however, without any doubt personal, dramatic, tragic experiences in his own suffering life. They were such deep, moving events that they led him to meditate over the 'despair of Man, taking Jesus as a symbol. At the beginning of September 1915, Oskar Kokoschka was so badly wounded on the Eastern Front that for a long time he was close to death. He came back to life with an experience that few have had. From the depths of that experience the magnificent music of Beethoven sounded with the words: Great is the agony, the anxiety, the terror . . . It is fear of oneself, of death, of eternity, of which the poets tell and which forms the very nucleus of this drama.

10 *Christus am Oelberg* (The Agony in the Garden). 1916. Black chalk. (20)

The artist derived the iconographical motif for the drawing from his background and in particular from Albrecht Altdorfer, whose altar piece in the Church of St Florian includes a miraculously evocative panel of the Agony in the Garden. The iconographic association with this historical image is clearly evident although the drawing does not bring to mind that landscape of the Danube School which is also the landscape of his childhood. Kokoschka's drawing retains with a slight variation the central figures of Christ and the Angel – adding with marked emphasis the dramatically drawn sky – while the group of mercenaries with Judas, which is in the background on the left in Altdorfer, is on the right of Kokoschka's composition. The group of sleeping disciples, however, is a fragment, the lower edge of the drawing having been irregularly torn off. We can still recognise the head of St Peter, leaning on his hand, and the body of another sleeper with his back to us but the rest is irrevocably lost. Yet this lost fragment in no way affects what is left. What is for us of the greatest significance is that the portrait of Christ is a self-portrait of the artist.

It is not uncommon for artists to portray themselves on panels of their works and they sometimes depict themselves as witnesses to important holy events. We can scarcely identify all the self-portraits which are hidden in the numerous anonymous figures represented in scenes from the Passion. But many of them are known to us; we recognise Grünewald in the figure of St Sebastian on the Isenheim Altarpiece, Dierick Bouts in that silent spectator, deep in thought, in the centre of the Last Supper of the splendid polyptich in the Church of St Peter in Louvain.

Only very rarely, however, does the artist paint himself with the face of Christ, Gauguin's wonderful *Agony in the Garden* of 1889 being another example. It was only with the highly developed individualism and subjectivism which emerged at the beginning of the 19th century that the artist dared to identify himself with Christ, an identification which would have probably been looked on as blasphemy or at least considered to be too daring a comparison in the Middle Ages.

The sufferings of Christ, interpreted as a symbol of agony, the physical pain and the mental torture of mankind allowed this type of comparison. We believe that this drawing by Oskar Kokoschka is a private expression of the agonies that he had suffered, of that unique feeling, anchored in half consciousness, of an existence on the border of being and not being.

This remarkable self-portrait has yet another significant feature which, although immediately clear, is made more obvious by a comparison with other self-portraits of the same period (1913, 1920). The face in the drawing of 1916 is not the portrait of a young man: it shows the features of a mature person whose face bears traces of a deep inner struggle and has aged in the process. This self-portrait, therefore, bears many of the characteristics of many other portraits done by Kokoschka: a transposition of time, a view of the sitter as he will look in the future. That clairvoyance so often attributed to Kokoschka is present – a clairvoyance which enabled the artist to visualise how a face would look years in the future and to capture the expressions which Life and Fate would impose upon his models' features.

This self-portrait of the thirty year old hidden under a mask of Jesus Christ obviously played a unique role in the work of Oskar Kokoschka. This bold identification with Christ in his ultimate agony is of exceptional significance in his work. Proof of this is also provided by Kokoschka's dedication on the drawing to the man who retrieved this work after more than fifty years of oblivion.

Kunštát na Morave, *November 1970*

NOTE

1. For another from this series see E. Rathenau, *Oskar Kokoschka Handzeichnungen 1906–1965*, Berlin and New York, 1966, pl. 42.

Kokoschka's late graphic work: A publisher's view
Bernhard Baer

Kokoschka's graphic work in its first great period, which contained *Tubutsch*, *Hiob*, *Der gefesselte Columbus*, culminated in *Bachkantate*. The words of the *Kantate* were the point of departure, but its content was autobiographical, an allegorical drama without words. To be confronted with this great work again at the Tate Gallery exhibition of 1962 after the long interval of war and postwar was a lightning revelation. Nothing comparable to these scenes, which raise passion and suffering to cosmic significance, had been done by the artist since or by any of his contemporaries. The *beaux livres* of the school of Paris – however beautiful – use words as a pretext for the display of graphic work rather than for a response to their content. Kokoschka's own gift as a playwright, poet, storyteller show the dual roots of his creative imagination. What makes Kokoschka the unique portrait painter in his generation, his grasp and insight which integrates the sitter into his vision, also gives him the profound response to literature. In his portraits he makes the sitter part of his own world of imagination – so to speak recreates him in his own image, which may explain the family likeness between his portraits. Equally so he identifies with the characters, situations, tensions of plays and poetry to recreate them in visual terms. It was thus that the encounter with *Bachkantate* at the Tate exhibition, the impact of a meeting after a long absence, moved me to approach Kokoschka with the suggestion of creating a suite of lithographs inspired by *King Lear*. I wrote

> 'Obviously we do not think of any literal form of illustration, but rather of evocations of the feeling, tensions and passions of this great tragedy.'

While I knew of Kokoschka's interest in Shakespeare, I wondered whether he would agree to link his work with a masterpiece of the past, when previously he mostly based it on his own ideas and writings or those of his friends and contemporaries like Ehrenstein and Karl Kraus. These doubts were dispelled at the first meeting. During a discussion which lasted the whole afternoon and ranged from the characters of the play to the format of the lithographs and the choice of the printer, Kokoschka told me of his English master at school and his early interest in Shakespeare. He concluded '*King Lear*, that thrills me – come back in three days time'. At this second meeting he showed me the first drawing, Edgar as a beggar, to whom he had given his own features – as later on he gave another version of his features to Lear. The Edgar drawing was at once taken to Wolfensberger in Zurich, who transferred it to the stone and proofed it. Kokoschka was pleased with the result and in a surge of creativity – he was then seventy-seven years old – he drew fourteen lithographs in less than six weeks. Of two of these he drew alternative versions, i.e. of the scene with the fool in the hovel and of Lear carrying the body of Cordelia. One crucial scene was still missing, the catharsis of the play, Lear's prayer in the storm. It followed after a break of three weeks: an image spiritually profound and of the most original invention, Lear rising out of the ground, his face unearthly, seen against the background of an apocalyptic storm (pl. 11). Like all the images, this is not a representation of a scene on the stage of a theatre, it is a visionary response to the essence of the play. Kokoschka combined the closest reading of the text with the greatest freedom of imagery. Edmund appears opposite the passage in which he reflects on his fortune in a self-revealing monologue. Everything mentioned in the text, the parents compounding him, the signs of the Zodiac, the chariot of the Sun is integrated in a baroque sweep around the figure of Edmund, bent on treachery and adventure, glowing with demonic attraction. Kokoschka commented that like Goneril and Regan in the play all women who saw the drawing fell in love with him. The speed of Kokoschka's

11 *King Lear: Lear*. 1963. Lithograph. (58·7)

creation inspired all concerned with the making of the book including the Oxford University Press, who set the type by hand and printed it in the traditional manner on moistened sheets. Ten months after the first meeting I could submit to Kokoschka a complete bound volume.

Lithography is Kokoschka's preferred medium. It is the most direct graphic process, a drawing made printable by the use of the litho crayon. As in his paintings Kokoschka aims at setting down spontaneously what moves his eye and his mind. This explains the rarity of coloured prints in his graphic work, which require separate drawings for each colour and the register of superimposed plates to take care of – technicalities which irk and worry him. When I once suggested the use of a second colour – in no sense as a realistic device – Kokoschka refused:

> 'It may not be difficult for artists who are working in the decorative French way; I would have to design on two sheets or stones at the same time. Each stroke on one of the drawings would have to be woven into the corresponding one of the other as in a tapestry. It would hamper my imagination and spontaneity.'

Quite literally Kokoschka has no time for graphic processes which require step by step development. He resents the delay caused by technical difficulties. Hence his avoidance of true etching (*eau forte*) which involves waiting for the acid to bite into the metal, he uses dry point instead, the direct drawing into the copper plate.

The spontaneity of the working does not exclude preparation or correction. Kokoschka told me that he had used idea sketches for the first time for *King Lear* and subsequently for *The Odyssey* and *Saul and David*. He used these sketches as stepping stones, a kind of visual scaffolding for the composition before attempting the final version; they are usually just the noting down of an idea. The final version is an entirely spontaneous development, never a copy. It is unthinkable for Kokoschka to square up a drawing for transfer into another size or another medium. The conception is meditated upon, the setting down is intuitive. Once the drawing has been transferred to the stone Kokoschka makes careful revisions, alteration of small details, the build-up of shadows for greater emphasis, as between the proof and the final version of the helmet in *The Women of Troy*. The wonderful poetic prologue to *The Odyssey* a drawing with the grasshopper and the lizard, contained a snail in its first version which the artist subsequently eliminated. He lavishes minute care on the works he put into the world in spontaneous creations.

Writing about the great Zurich exhibition on the occasion of his 80th birthday Kokoschka remarked:

> 'Like at the Tate the result for me was a certain sadness that such a short life had passed so quickly. As a diary it seems to be unique.'

Of course, the work of great artists seen over a long period must reveal something of their personality. In Kokoschka the urge for self-revelation was clear from his early work, from *The Tempest* and *Knight Errant*, the range of self-portraits, *Bachkantate* and *Columbus Bound* to the great cycles of his late work. Here is what he has to say himself:

> 'I loved my Odyssey and while drawing the pictures felt perfectly identified with the hero.'

Or again:

> 'I could identify myself with this figure Odysseus as a Vagabond, as an eternal wanderer.'

Kokoschka revelled in the thought that Odysseus, having returned after an absence of twenty years, left home again after one night in the bed he had built. The scope of the work, as at first planned, was the return of Odysseus from the landing at Ithaca. But Kokoschka had become so deeply involved with the figure of Odysseus, that he decided to go back to the beginning and to encompass the whole of the *Odyssey*. In the end he wrote with regret:

> 'Odysseus has become a human being to me with many adventures, inner development. He lives. He has gone away and leaves me with the pain of separation.'

A similar identification moved him when he worked on *Saul and David*. He described the theme as a Janus head – seeing himself as an old man in Saul, as a young man in David:

> 'Saul is furious at being eighty as I am. He cannot grasp the fact that he is now eighty as yesterday he was only eighteen – like David who is standing behind him – it seems only yesterday I was eighteen.'

Kokoschka's thought and vision throughout his life were concerned with human values. The striving for the absolute, for the significant form are entirely alien to his genius. This sets him apart from his contemporaries whose work is rooted in the School of Paris. No painter of this school could have conceived the mythical self-revealing compositions nor the cosmic landscapes, nor the gallery of great portraits, which are unique in the oeuvre of artists of Kokoschka's generation. It was a total comprehension which enabled him to create images of Cordelia's death, of Eurycleia's recognition, of Saul calling out for David. The same insights and impulses are behind his response to Greek antiquity. It has been remarked that so much of Kokoschka's late work has been inspired by Greek themes – *Hellas, Apulia, The Odyssey, The Women of Troy*, the Thermopylae paintings – as nothing in his earlier work seemed to relate to Greek art. The artist himself explained in many utterances what drew him to Greek civilisation. To him the past is not something closed, seen from a great distance, which has to be reconstructed. Kokoschka evokes it, because it is alive to him. He makes the Greek statue come to life – a modern Pygmalion – in the terms of his vision. The small terracotta medallion becomes a living breathing girl, the fragment of the dog from the Acropolis an animal ready to jump (pl. 23). The magic extends to much more humble objects; the papier-mâché toy in his studio takes on life as a ferocious tiger in a lithograph.

He shares the power of the greatest artist to make the word image, to arrest the fleeting moment, to make the past present. What he gives us is summed up in one word of the poet: 'soulenliv'ning'.

Catalogue

The catalogue raisonné numbers (ww) refer to Hans Wingler and Friedrich Welz's fully illustrated *O. Kokokschka – Das druckgraphische Werk*, Galerie Welz, Salzburg, 1975.

Lithographs and etchings are printed in black, and the inscriptions are in the same medium as the image, unless otherwise stated.

The dimensions are given in centimetres, height preceding width. They refer to the size of the drawn area, or in the case of etchings, the size of the platemark, unless otherwise stated.

Illustrations are indicated by an asterisk.

1 *Und das Wort ist Fleisch geworden*   (ww 1) (And the word was made flesh)
Book-plate of Dr Lorenz Kellner, 1906. Signed and dated in ink *OK 06*. Woodcut. 13·5 ×8·5.
This is the only woodcut in Kokoschka's oeuvre. Dr Lorenz Kellner was Kokoschka's teacher of English.

2 *Madonna*
Design for the book-plate of Frau Emma Bacher, 1906. On the back is another design for a book-plate *Man, deer and flowers*. Pencil and black ink. 12·5 ×11

3 *Lovers*
Design for the book-plate of Frau Emma Bacher, 1906. On the back is another design for a book-plate *Still life, pineapple, flowers and an exotic bird*. Pencil and black ink. 11·5 ×8·5

4 *Three girls with sheafs of corn*
Book-plate of Frau Emma Bacher, 1907. Signed *OK*, and again in pencil at a later date *OKokoschka*. Probably line-block. 7·4 ×5·9

5 *Three angels over a cornfield*
Probably intended as a book-plate. c.1907. Signed *OK*. Dated in pencil *um 1907*. Probably line-block. 7·2 ×7

6 Book-plate of Mitzi and Dr Josef Binder, 1911. Signed *OK*. Line-block. 10·2 ×6·4

7 Book-plate of Dr Robert Freund, 1911. Signed *OK*. Line-block. 8 ×5·5

8 Book-plate of Frau Dr Lotte Franzos, 1911. Signed *OK*. Line-block. 5·8 ×6·7

9 Book-plate of Lily and Arthur Fürst, 1911. Signed *OK* and again *OKokoschka fecit*. Line-block. 4·3 ×3·2

10 Design for a book-plate, 1911. Signed *OK*. Pen and ink. 6·8 ×7·9

This drawing incorporates the designs for both Lotte Franzos's and Robert Freund's book-plates (see nos. 7 & 8).

11 Eighteen postcards, including three variations, published by the Wiener Werkstätte 1906–1908. Each signed *OK*. Colour lithographs. Each card 14·1 ×9
  Reiter und Segelschiff (Rider and   (ww 3) sailing ship) (Postcard no. 55)
  Blumengarten (Flower garden) (Post-   (ww 4) card no. 64). With variation, lettered *Herzlichen Gruss*
  Jäger und Tiere (Huntsman and prey)   (ww 5) (Postcard no. 72)
  Flötenspieler und Fledermäuse (Flaut-   (ww 6) ist and bats) (Postcard no. 73)
  Biedermeierdame auf Wiese (Lady in   (ww 7) a meadow) (Postcard no. 76)
  Mädchen mit Lamm, von Räubern   (ww 8) *bedroht* (Girl with lamb, threatened by brigands) (Postcard no. 77)
  Musikanten (Musicians) (Postcard no.   (ww 9) 78)
  Mädchen mit Schaf auf Bergwiese   (ww 10) (Girl with sheep in mountain-pasture) (Postcard no. 79)
  Sennerin und Kuh (Dairy-maid and   (ww 11) cow) (Postcard no. 80)
  Drei Hirten, Hund und Schafe (Three   (ww 12) shepherds, dog and sheep) (Postcard no. 116)
  Mutter mit drei Kindern (Mother   (ww 13) with three children) (Postcard no. 117)
  Drei Mädchen, Lamm und Paradies-   (ww 14) *vögel* (Three girls, lamb and birds of Paradise) (Postcard no. 147) With variation, lettered *Froehliches Osterfest*
  Mädchen am Fenster (Girl at a win-   (ww 15) dow) (Postcard no. 152)
  Die Heiligen Drei Könige (The   (ww 16) Three Kings) (Postcard no. 155)
  Mädchen auf Wiese vor einem Dorf   (ww 17) (Girl in a meadow in front of a village) (Postcard no. 157). With variation, lettered *Froehliches Osterfest*

Between 1906 and 1914 the Wiener Werkstätte published over 900 postcards in a numbered series.

12 Programme of the 'Fledermaus'   (ww 20) Cabaret, Vienna*
Issued at its opening, October 1907. Inscribed in pencil inside the front cover *Früh tritt der brave Bethusy den OK an* (*bin noch verschlafen . . .*) *OKokoschka 1974*. Showing *Hirsch, Fuchs und Zauberer* (Stag, fox and magician), an illustration by Kokoschka to his shadow play *Das getupfte Ei* (The speckled egg), which formed part of the entertainment. Signed *OK*. Colour lithograph. Image without border 14·8 ×15·1

The decorated border was designed by C. O. Czeschka

13 *Die Träumenden Knaben* (The (ww 22-29) Dreaming Youths)
Reprint published by Verlag Jugend und Volk, Vienna, Munich, May 1968. Lyrical prose poem, written by Kokoschka in 1907 and dedicated to Gustav Klimt, originally published by the Wiener Werkstätte, 1908, with two black and white illustrations and eight colour lithographs. Inscribed on the fly-leaf with dedication *für den immer treuen Grafen Reinhold Bethusy-Huc mit freundlichen Gedanken Oskar Kokoschka 30.V.69.* Photo-lithographs. 24 × 28·5
Open showing *Schlafende Frau* (Sleep- (ww 22) ing woman)

14 Poster advertising an exhibition of Kokoschka's 'aquarelles, oeuvres graphiques' held at the Musée d'art moderne de la ville de Paris, 26 September to 17 November 1974. Reproducing the lithograph *Pietà* (ww 31), designed as a poster in 1908 and published by the Internationale Kunstschau, Vienna, 1909. Colour offset. Size of sheet 109 × 57

15 *Der Sturm*
Five issues of the art periodical published by Herwarth Walden, Berlin, 1910–1932, containing reproductions of Kokoschka's series of portrait drawings *Menschenköpfe*. Each portrait signed *OK*. Line-block and letterpress.
  Karl Kraus. No. 12, 19 May 1910.* 29·2 × 24
  Adolf Loos. No. 18, 30 June 1910. 28 × 25·5
  Herwarth Walden. No. 22, 28 July 1910.* 24·2 × 18·4
  Yvette Guilbert. No. 70, July 1911.* 23·2 × 19·7
  Rudolf Blümner. Part 7, October 1916. 30 × 19·5
The complete series consisted of 15 portraits, which were reprinted and published as a set in 1916 (see no. 19).

16 *Zwanzig Zeichnungen*
Four from the portfolio of twenty reproductions of Kokoschka's drawings, published by *Der Sturm*, Berlin, 1913. The title-page signed and dated in pencil *OKokoschka 1913*. Each drawing signed in facsimile *OK*. Line-blocks. Size of sheets 42 × 30·5
  (7 & 8) Illustrations (2) to Kokoschka's play *Mörder Hoffnung der Frauen* (Murderer Hope of Women)
  (11) *Himmlische und irdische Liebe* (Heavenly and earthly love)
  (14) *Die schöne Rollschuhläuferin* (The beautiful roller-skater)
All the drawings from this portfolio had been published previously in the periodical *Der Sturm* (See no. 15)

17 Karl Kraus, *Die chinesische* (ww 35-42) *Mauer* (The Chinese Wall)*
Published by Kurt Wolff, Leipzig, 1914, with eight lithographs made by Kokoschka in 1913. Edition of 200. Each lithograph signed *OK* and again in pencil *OKokoschka.*

Open showing *Die Eindringlinge* (The (ww 42) Intruders)

18 Herwarth Walden, *Die Judentochter* (The Jew's Daughter)
Song-book with title-page illustrated by Kokoschka, published by *Der Sturm*, Berlin, 1916. Signed *OK*. Probably line-block, coloured by hand. 30·5 × 24

19 *Menschenköpfe*
Three from the portfolio of fifteen reproductions of Kokoschka's portrait drawings published by *Der Sturm*, Berlin, 1916. Each signed *OK*. Line-blocks. Size of sheets 42 × 30·2
  (4) *Richard Dehmel*
  (14) *Gertrud Eysoldt*. Inscribed and dated *Frau Eysoldt 1916.*
  (15) *Clair Waldoff*

20 *Christus am Oelberg* (The Agony in the Garden)*
Drawing for the series on the theme of 'The Passion' in the periodical *Der Bildermann* Berlin, 1916, but not used as a lithograph (see no. 21). Inscribed on the mount with the dedication *20 Jahre lang kennen wir uns, lieber Graf Bethusy und noch finden Sie solche köstliche verlorene Dinge, ich danke Ihnen von Herzen Ihr OKokoschka 1.V.70* Black chalk. 36 × 31

21 *Die Passion* (The Passion) (ww 78-83)
Two from the series of six lithographs on the theme of 'The Passion', published in the periodical *Der Bildermann*, edited and published by Paul Cassirer, Berlin, 1916. Size of sheets 28 × 35
  Christus am Kreuz (Christ on the (ww 80) Cross), 20 September 1916. Signed *Kokoschka.*
  Der Judaskuss (*Gefangennahme* (ww 82) *Christi*) (The Kiss of Judas), 20 November 1916. Signed *OK*.

22 *Der Traum* (The Dream) (ww 86)
Illustration to Act 4, Scene 1 of *The Tempest* from a portfolio entitled *Shakespeare-Visionen*, drawn 1916–17 and published for the Marées-Gesellschaft by R. Piper & Co., Munich, 1918. Signed *OK* and inscribed *We are such stuff as dreams are made on, and our little life is rounded with a sleep . . .* Signed in pencil *OKokoschka*. Lithograph. 26·5 × 23·8
At least 30 artists contributed to this portfolio.

23 Oskar Kokoschka, *Hiob* (Job)* (ww 87-100)
De luxe edition with fourteen lithographs by Kokoschka, dedicated to Fritz Neuberger, and published by Paul Cassirer, Berlin, 1917. Numbered *33* and in pencil *von 90.* Signed in pencil *Oskar Kokoschka.* Open showing the first illustration, printed in red:
Adam and Eve. (ww 87)
The original version of this drama was written in 1907 and given the title *Sphinx und Strohmann*. It was published in *Dramen und Bilder*, Leipzig, 1913. A later edition, with the title *Hiob*, but without the illustrations, was published by Cassirer in

1919. The play was first produced by the author's colleagues at the Wiener Werkstätte in 1907. It was also produced at the 'Fledermaus' Cabaret in 1911, and by the Cabaret Voltaire as part of the second 'Sturm' soirée at the Dada Gallery in Zurich, 14 April 1917.

24 Victor von Dirsztay, *Lob des* (ww 104-109)
hohen Verstandes (In Praise of Pure Reason)
With a title-vignette and six lithographs by Kokoschka, published by Kurt Wolff, Leipzig, 1917. Inscribed in ink with the dedication from the author *Baron LW. Rothschild mit herzlichen Empfehlung gewidmet vom Verfasser. März 1930 Wien. XVIII Plenergasse 24. Atelier.* Each lithograph signed *OK* and again in pencil *O Kokoschka.* Open showing the first illustration: *Den Strick bloss zu beschaffen* (The bare rope is (ww 104) effective).

25 *Romana Kokoschka* (Mother of (ww 110)
the artist)
Published by Paul Cassirer, Berlin, 1917. Total edition of 80. From the edition of 30 on Japan paper. Signed. Lithograph. 28·9 ×21·4

26 *Dr Fritz Neuberger* (ww 111)
Published by Paul Cassirer, Berlin, 1917. Edition of 100. Lithograph. 38·5 ×27·5
Kokoschka met Dr Fritz Neuberger in the winter of 1916 and became close friends with a group of artists this philosopher and writer had gathered around him in Dresden. The artist's play *Hiob* (see no. 23) is dedicated to him. Neuberger died of consumption in 1923.

27 *Corona I** (ww 126)
Drawn 1918 and published by Paul Cassirer, Berlin, 1919. Edition of 50. Signed and dated in pencil *Oskar Kokoschka 1918.* Lithograph. 55·7 ×43

28 *Katia* (ww 133)
Drawn 1918 and published by Paul Cassirer, Berlin, 1919. Edition of 75. Inscribed and signed *Katia OK* and signed again in pencil *O Kokoschka.* Lithograph, printed in blue. 69·3 ×49·9
The actress, Käthe Richter, was one of Kokoschka's favourite models. In addition to this portrait, he made two other lithographic portraits of her. She appears in four of his paintings and was the model for the lithograph *The rest on the flight into Egypt* (ww 84). She played the lead in a number of his plays and *Der Brennende Dornbusch* (The Burning Bush) published in *Vier Dramen,* Paul Cassirer, 1919, is dedicated to her.

29 *Max Reinhardt** (ww 136)
Published by Paul Cassirer, Berlin, 1919. Edition of 125. Signed in pencil *O Kokoschka.* Lithograph. 62·5 ×47·3
In 1919 Kokoschka drew two lithographic portraits of the stage director and producer, Max Reinhardt (1873–1943). During the same year his play *Hiob* (see no. 23) was produced at Reinhardt's Kammerspiele, Berlin.

30 *Hermine Körner* (ww 138)
Published by Paul Cassirer, Berlin, 1920. Edition of 125. Proof of the second state. Signed in pencil *O Kokoschka* and inscribed *Litho Probedruck.* Lithograph, printed in blue. 67·7 ×47·5
Kokoschka met Hermine Körner (1898–1960), a leading actress of the Expressionist generation, in Dresden and Berlin.

31 *Das Konzert* (The Concert) (ww 140-144)
Four from the series of five lithographs published by Paul Cassirer, Berlin, 1921. Each signed in pencil *O Kokoschka.*
    *Das Konzert I (Naemi).** Printed in (ww 140)
orange. 69·8 ×46·7
    Das Konzert II (Hagar). Numbered (ww 141)
48/100. 66·7 ×48·5
    Das Konzert IV (Mirjam). Num- (ww 143)
bered *41/100.* 69·3 ×49·1
    Das Konzert V (Deborah). Edition (ww 144)
of 100. Inscribed *Wenn Camilla Beethoven gehört hat O Kokoschka Villeneuve 1920.* 68·4 ×52·3
In 1920 Kokoschka made a series of over 20 drawings of Camilla Swoboda, wife of the Viennese art historian, Karl Maria Swoboda. The five published as lithographs in the series entitled *Das Konzert* were also used in the series of 10 lithographs entitled *Die Töchter des Bundes* (The Daughters of the Covenant), published by Paul Cassirer, 1921–1922. Ten of the drawings were reproduced in facsimile in *Variationen über ein Thema* (see no. 32). The exhibited images were nos. 3, 10, 6 and 5 respectively in this portfolio.

32 *Variationen über ein Thema* (Variations on a Theme)
Five (nos. 1, 4, 7, 8 and 9) from the portfolio of ten facsimiles of drawings by Kokoschka, with a foreword by Max Dvořák, edited by Bohuslav Kokoschka, published by Richard Lanyi, Vienna, and Ed. Strache, Vienna, Prague and Leipzig, 1921. Dedicated in blue chalk on the back of the title-page: *Dem verehrten Herren Dr. Schwarzmann mit freundlichsten Gedanken zugeeignet Oskar Kokoschka Wien 29.V.24.* Each facsimile stamped on the back with number. Collotype. Size of sheets 70 ×50

33 Oskar Kokoschka and Paul Hindemith, *Mörder Hoffnung der Frauen,* (Murderer Hope of Women), Op. 12. Piano-score of Hindemith's opera, with words by Kokoschka, based on his play of the same title. Published by S. Schott's Söhne, Mainz, 1921. Inscribed in pencil beneath a photograph of the composer '*Soll er nur Komponieren' schrieb ich damals als ich seine Composition genehmigte O Kokoschka.*

34 *Der Künstler und die Muse* (The artist and his Muse)*
Matrix for a plaque of the Dresden Artists' Association, 1922. Front lettered *ANIMA;* back, *MANIA.* Painted plaster relief. Circular, diameter 11·2
Another version of this plaque, made in porcelain

by the Staatliche Porzellanmanufaktur, is reproduced in H. W. Wingler, *Oskar Kokoschka the work of the painter*, Salzburg, 1958, p. 338, no. D 13. It has a different design on the face lettered 'Anima'.

35 *Ruth II** (ww 153)
Published by Paul Cassirer, Berlin, 1922. Signed in pencil *OKokoschka* and numbered *100/176*. Lithograph. 45·9 × 37·4
Issued in the series *Die Töchter des Bundes* (The Daughters of the Covenant) (see no. 31). Ruth Landshoff (1904–1966), the daughter of an actress, went on the stage herself and later became a writer.

36 *Lily Christiansen-Agoston* (ww 157)
Probably published by Fritz Gurlitt, Berlin, 1922. Signed in pencil *Litho O Kokoschka*. Inscribed and dated by the sitter *Eipperchen, dem treuen Kollegen in Freud und Leid zur Erinnerung an Lily 6.IV.20 – 6.IV.22 – 10.VII.22*. Lithograph. 48·3 × 52·2
Lily Christiansen-Agoston (1894–1950) was an actress.

37 *Maria Orska* (ww 158)
Published by Paul Cassirer, Berlin, 1922. Signed in pencil *OKokoschka* and numbered *16/247*. Lithograph. 55·9 × 39·9
Maria Orska (1893/4–1930) was an actress.

38 *Self-portrait from two aspects* (ww 164)
Poster for the Kokoschka exhibition held at the Kunstsalon Wolfsberger, Zurich, September–October 1923. Signed and dated in pencil at a later date *OKokoschka 1923*. Colour lithograph. Size of sheet 127·5 × 91·4

39 Oskar Kokoschka and Ernst Křenek, *Orpheus und Eurydike*, Op. 21. Piano-score of Křenek's opera, with words by Kokoschka, based on his play of the same title. Published by Universal-Edition, Vienna and New York, 1973. First published 1925. Signed in pencil *OKokoschka* and dedicated in ink by the composer *Für Reinhold, Count Bethusy-Huc zur guten Erinnerung an die Grazer Aufführung Ernst Krenek 20. Oct. 1973*.

40 Bohuslav Kokoschka, *Geh,* (ww 167, 168)
mach die Tür zu, es zieht! (Close the door will you, there is a draught). Published by the Johannes-Presse, Vienna, 1926. From the edition of 33 with two illustrations by Oskar Kokoschka, the author's brother, interleaved. Inscribed in ink with a dedication from the author: *Freund Bethusy mit den herzlichsten Grüssen, Weihnachten 1974 Bohuslav Kokoschka*.
   Hahn, eine Henne tretend (Cock (ww 167)
   mounting a hen)
   Illustration for the title-page. 1925–1926. Signed in pencil *Oskar Kokoschka*. Dry-point, printed in brown, on India paper. 11 × 13·6
   Zwei Menschen (Two people) (ww 168)
   Illustration to face page 32. 1925–1926. Signed in pencil *Oskar Kokoschka*. Dry-point on India paper. 21 × 17·6

41 *Empfang König David* (Hail, King David)
1928. Inscribed and signed *Touggourt OK*. Inscribed on the mount at a later date with title and *OKokoschka 1926*. Pencil. 20·5 × 26
This drawing was made during the second half of February 1928 while Kokoschka was travelling in North Africa. He had just finished his painting *Exodus* near Biskra and went by train to Touggourt, where he painted *The Marabut of Temacin*.

42 *Trudl* (ww 171)
1931. Signed *OK* and again in pencil *OKokoschka*. Lithograph, printed in red. 31·5 × 24
The model was an eleven year old Viennese girl who sat for four of Kokoschka's paintings as well as being the model for about 20 drawings.

43 *Trudl mit Strohhut* (Trudl with (ww 173)
straw hat)*
1931. Signed in pencil *OKokoschka*. Lithograph, printed in red. 35·2 × 43·4

44 K. B. Palkovský, *Svitani* (ww 176-179)
(Daybreak)
Type-script of the play in the original Czech, 1939, with a German translation entitled *Morgendaemmerung*. With four etched illustrations by Kokoschka and photographs of his preliminary sketches, 1942. Text with dedication from the author *Meinem lieben Freund Reinhold freundschaftlich K. B. Palkovský Praha 6.8.1973*.
   (1) *Dorfschenke* (Village inn) 10·4 (ww 176)
   × 14·9
   (2) *Dorfgericht* (Village court) 11 × (ww 177)
   14·9
   (3) *Szene am Ufer* (Scene on the (ww 178)
   shore) 10·4 × 14·9
   (4) *Schlittenpartie* (Sledging-party) (ww 179)
   11 × 15
Kokoschka first met Palkovský in 1914 in Vienna. They met again in 1935 when Kokoschka moved to Prague and Palkovský later became his father-in-law. Madame Lida Palkovska translated *Svitani* into German for Kokoschka in 1942. This set of proofs of the illustrations was made in London. It is not one of the 'Salzburg' sets recorded by Wingler and Welz.

45 *In Memory of the Children of* (ww 180)
*Europe who have to die of cold and hunger this Xmas**
Poster, 1945. Signed *OK*. Signed and dated in ink *Original Litho Oskar Kokoschka London Dez. 45*. Lithograph. 61 × 48
Five thousand copies of this poster were displayed in London as an appeal by the Artist for the starving children of Europe.

46 Bohuslav Kokoschka, *Logbuch des B.K.*
Published by Franz Ehrenwirth, Munich, 1972. Completed under the title *Ketten in das Meer* (Chains into the sea) in 1919, but not published. With eight reproductions of drawings illustrating the novel, made by Oskar Kokoschka, (brother of the author) in 1947, but never published. Book with dedication *Ein Buch! Geschenkt am Tage des*

Erscheinens, R.Bethusy-Huc, geschrieben aber schon vor fünfzig Jahren! Doch was damals mich umdrängte, der guten und der bösen Geister Scharen, ob wir sie nun hassen oder lieben, ob aus dem Licht sie oder aus dem Dunkel waren, bis heute sind die gleichen sie geblieben! 22.Nov.1972 Bohuslav Kokoschka.

47 *Olda Kokoschka* (The artist's (ww 183)
wife)*
Issued with the de luxe edition of Michelangelo Masciotta's *Oskar Kokoschka*, published by Del Turco, Florence, 1949. Signed in pencil *Oskar Kokoschka* and numbered *22/55*. Dry-point. 20·8 × 14·6

48 *Leda mit dem Schwan* (Leda with (ww 184)
the swan)
Published by Rudolf Hoffmann, Hamburg, 1951. Inscribed and signed in reverse *hommage à Sèvres OK*. Signed in pencil *O Kokoschka* and numbered *1/15*. Lithograph, printed in umber. 32·6 × 32·2

49 *Die magische Form (Der Zauberer)* (ww 185)
(The Magic Form, the Magician)
Published by Rudolf Hoffmann, Hamburg, 1951. Signed in pencil *OKokoschka* and numbered *6/15*. Lithograph, printed in dark olive. 50·5 × 37
This print shows the artist as a shadow-play magician. There is a painting of the same composition in reverse.

50 *Der Fuchs und die sauren Trauben* (ww 186)
(The Fox and the Grapes)
Illustration to La Fontaine's fable, published by the Guilde de la Gravure, Geneva, 1952. Edition of 200. Signed in pencil *OKokoschka*. Colour lithograph. 40·9 × 55·3

51 *Windhund* (Greyhound) (ww 187)
Published by the Guilde de la Gravure, Geneva, 1952. Printed by Emil Matthieu, Zurich, in an edition of 200. Signed in pencil *OKokoschka*. Colour lithograph. 37·3 × 63

52 *Amor und Psyche* (ww 205)
Published by Galerie Beyeler, Basel, 1955. Edition of 70. Proof. Signed and inscribed *Probeandruck OKokoschka Xmas Villeneuve 73*. Colour lithograph. 58·5 × 51·3
This print has the same composition in reverse as Kokoschka's painting of the same subject begun in 1950 and completed in 1955. The composition was also produced as a tapestry by the Wiener Gobelin-Manufaktur, Vienna, during 1956.

53 *Self-portrait* (ww 206)
Published by Galerie Welz, Salzburg, 1956. Signed and dated in pencil *OKokoschka 1956* and numbered *6/90*. Colour lithograph. 58·2 × 42
An edition of 19 of this lithograph was published in black also.

54 *L'Enfant de Bethléem* (ww 209)
Published by Schweizer Lithographenbund, 1956. Signed *OKokoschka* and inscribed with title and dated *1956*. Signed and dated in pencil *Pr. Dr. Litho OK 56*. Colour lithograph. 50·5 × 42·7
Given by the artist to the Help for Hungary Campaign.

55 *Dornengekrönter Christus* (Christ (ww 210)
crowned with thorns)
Published by Woldemar Klein, Baden-Baden, 1956. Signed in pencil *Litho. OKokoschka* and numbered *61/65*. Lithograph. 53·9 × 38·8
Given by the artist to the Help for Hungary Campaign.

56 *Hamburger Hafen* (The harbour (ww 216)
at Hamburg)
Published by the Vereinigung Griffelkunst, Hamburg-Langenhorn, 1961. Edition of 50. Proof. Signed and dated *OK 61*. Signed and dated and inscribed in pencil *Probe druck OKokoschka 61*. Lithograph, printed in brownish green. 46 × 61
Hamburg is viewed from the river Elbe.

57 *Steigendes Pferd* (Prancing horse) (ww 220)
Published by Griffelkunst, Hamburg-Langenhorn, 1962. Signed and dated *OK 62*. Lithograph. 43·5 × 39
The drawing for this print was made from a T'ang sculpture.

58 *King Lear* (ww 223-238)
Five from the portfolio of 16 illustrations to Shakespeare's complete original text, published by Ganymed Original Editions Ltd, London, 1963. Edition of 275 with four additional copies. Each signed in pencil *OKokoschka*. Numbered on the colophon *168* and signed *OKokoschka Villeneuve 28.X.70*. Lithographs, printed in brown. Size of sheets 45·7 × 36·5
    (3) *Edmund.* 'This is excellent (ww 225)
foppery of the world'. Act I, Scene 2
    (6) *Lear, Regan, Goneril.* 'O reason (ww 228)
not the need'. Act II, Scene 3
    (7) *Lear.* 'Poor naked wretches'. (ww 229)
Act III, Scene 4.*
    (13) *Cordelia.* 'O you kind gods, (ww 235)
cure this great breach in his abused nature!'
Act IV, Scene 7
    (15) *Lear with Cordelia in his arms.* (ww 237)
'If that her breath will mist or stain the stone,
Why then she lives'. Act V, Scene 3

59 *Homage to Hellas* (ww 242-267)
Six lithographs from the two portfolios, each containing twelve lithographs and texts selected from ancient Greek literature by Edgar Horstmann, published by Marlborough Fine Art Ltd, London, 1964. Standard edition of 65 with a de luxe edition, containing two additional lithographs, of 15. Each signed in pencil *OKokoschka* and numbered *61/65*. Size of sheets 53 × 67·5
    (I.8) *Siren* (ww 249)
    (I.10) *Hygieia I* (ww 251)
    (I.11) *Shepherd's Dog** (ww 252)

(II.4) *Aegina II* (ww 258)
(II.6) *Acropolis II* (ww 260)
(II.13) *The blond Epheboi* (De luxe (ww 268)
edition addition)

60 *Apulian Journey* (ww 268-287)
Three from the suite of twenty lithographs drawn
in 1963 and published by Marlborough Fine Art
Ltd, London, 1964. Production supervised by
Ganymed Original Editions, London. Edition of
50. Size of sheets 51·5 ×66·8
  (4) *The Donkey Ciccio* (ww 271)
  Signed *OKokoschka*. Numbered *37/50*.
  (5) *Almond Trees* (ww 272)
  Signed in pencil *OKokoschka*.
  (20) *Cora* (ww 287)
  Signed in pencil *OKokoschka* and numbered
  2/50. Rare copy not issued in the standard
  edition.

61 *Fische, Langusten* (Fish, shrimps) (ww 290)
Drawn 1963. No edition published. Inscribed and
signed in pencil *Proof OKokoschka*. Lithograph.
35·5 ×66·4
In the vein of the *Apulia* lithographs, but not
included in the portfolio.

62 *Vier Schweine* (Four wild boar) (ww 291)
Drawn 1963. No edition published. Proof.
Lithograph. 27·5 ×48·4
See note to no. 61.

63 *Lizard and Grasshopper*
Signed and dated in black chalk *OKokoschka 64*
and inscribed *Villeneuve*. Water-colour. 36·5 ×37

64 *The Odyssey* (ww 294-338)
Six from the suite of 44 lithographs and a title-
vignette, each contained in a folio with quotations
from the text taken from Robert Fitzgerald's
translation. Drawn 1964–1965 and published
jointly by Marlborough Fine Art, London, and
Ganymed Original Editions Ltd, London, 1966.
Standard edition of 50, plus nine sets each with
original drawing, and four sets for the artist. Each
signed in pencil *OKokoschka* and numbered *14/50*.
Size of sheets 57 ×39·5
  (3) *Athena ready to depart for* (ww 297)
  Ithaka
  (12) *Kirke turning the men into* (ww 306)
  swine
  (17) *Skylla and Kharybdis* (ww 311)
  (34) *Eurykleia recognises Odysseus* (ww 328)
  (37) *Odysseus strings the bow* (ww 331)
  (39) *After the slaying of the suitors* (ww 333)

65 *Self-portrait** (ww 358)
Published by Kunstsalon Wolfsberg, Zurich, 1966.
Signed *OK*. Signed and dated in pencil *Litho
OKokoschka 1966*. With dedication *Für Reinhold
Graf Bethusy-Huc Zur Erinnerung an OK Villeneuve
31.5.69*. Numbered *VII/LXXV*. Lithograph, prin-
ted in red.
Also issued in black, in an edition of 50, and with
additional lettering, used as an exhibition poster
by the Galerie Welz, Salzburg, the Museum De
Lakenthal, Leiden, and the Kunstsalon Wolfsberg.

66 *Konrad Adenauer* (ww 359)
Published by Willy Hahn, Stuttgart, 1966. De luxe
edition of 35 plus five proofs and ten copies for the
artist. Standard edition of 45, plus five for the
artist. Signed and dated *OK 16.IV.66*. Signed in
pencil *OKokoschka* and numbered *III/XXV*. Lithograph. 40·5 ×34·5
Konrad Adenauer (1876–1967) was Chancellor of
West Germany from 1949 to 1963.

67 *Pegasus* (ww 360)
Published by the Kunsthaus, Zurich, 1966. Signed
OK and again in pencil *Oskar Kokoschka*. Num-
bered *27/100*. With dedication *Lieber Bethusy,
erinneren Sie Ihre liebe Frau Mutter in dieser
Ausstellung in Zürich 1966, ich sicher Ihr OK*.
Lithograph. 93 ×64
Also issued, with lettering, as a poster for the
Kokoschka exhibition held at the Kunsthaus,
Zurich.

68 *Le Bal masqué* (ww 367–373)
Four from the suite of seven colour lithographs
illustrating Verdi's opera *Un Ballo in Maschera*,
drawn 1965–1967, and published by Les Grands
Livres Illustrés Par Les Peintres Contemporains,
1967. With text by Marcel Jouhandeau. Edition
of 71, plus 12 sets for the artist, 38 sets for
collaborators and 34 sets without text. The set
numbered *XX* and signed in pencil *Félia Léal
Marcel Jouhandeau* and *OKokoschka*. Each lithograph signed in pencil *OK*. Size of sheets, folded
52·5 ×75·5
  (1) *Le Cerf, le Cygne sont des* (ww 367)
  masques . . .
  (3) *Pour moi, notre physionomie* (ww 369)
  réelle . . .
  (4) *L'Enlèvement est un symbole . . .* (ww 370)
  (6) *Les Perspectives de la Mort . . .* (ww 372)
Kokoschka designed the sets for a production of
this opera in the Teatro Communale, Florence, in
1962.

69 *Manhattan I* (ww 375)
From a portfolio of five lithographs, drawn 1966,
and published by Marlborough Fine Art, London,
1967. Signed *OK* and again in pencil *OKokoschka*.
Numbered *74/75*. 57·7 ×63·7

70 *El Djem* (ww 379)
Drawn 1967. Published by J. E. Wolfensberger,
Zurich, 1971. Signed in pencil *OKokoschka* and
numbered *1/50*. Lithograph. 47·7 ×66·4
A view of the amphitheatre at El Djem, Tunisia,
which Kokoschka visited in 1967.

71 *Saul and David* (ww 392-432)
Four from the suite of 41 lithographs each con-
tained in a folio with text from the Old Testament.
Drawn 1965–1968 and published by Marlborough
Fine Art, London, in association with Ganymed
Original Editions Ltd, London, 1969. Standard
edition of 60, plus six sets each with original
drawing and four sets (A-D) for the artist. Each
signed in pencil *OKokoschka* and numbered *1/60*.
Size of sheets 44·5 ×35

(4) *The Spirit of God came upon* (ww 395)
Saul
(13) *David hiding himself* * (ww 404)
(26) *David dancing before the ark* (ww 417)
(39) *David in his old age* * (ww 430)

72 *Longévité* (ww 436)
Published by the Swiss Centre for Clinical Research into Tumours, Tiefenau Hospital, Bern, 1968. Edition of 125, plus five for the artist. Proof. Signed and dated *O Kokoschka 1968* and inscribed with title. Inscribed in pencil *gut zum Druck OK*. Lithograph. 47·5 × 39·2

73 *Kouros I* (ww 449)
Drawn 1968 and published by Edition Olympia 1972 GmbH, Munich, 1970. From a set of 27 proofs. Signed in pencil *O Kokoschka*. Colour serigraph. 94·1 × 60·5

74 *Kouros II* (ww 450)
Drawn 1968 and published 1970. Signed *O Kokoschka* and again in pencil. Numbered *41/70*. Lithograph, printed in brown. 89 × 50·3

75 *Self-portrait* (ww 468)
1970. Issued with the first and second de luxe editions of Kokoschka's *Dichtung und Dramen*, volume 1 of *Das Schriftliche Werk*, edited by Heinz Spielmann and published by Hans Christians, Hamburg, 1973. Total edition of 152. From the first edition. Signed in pencil *O Kokoschka* and numbered *1/40*. Dry-point. 15·3 × 9·2

76 *Self-portrait with tortoise* (ww 465)
Drawn 1969 and published by Cercle Graphique Européen, 1970. Edition of 200. Proof. Signed and dated *O Kokoschka 12.12.69*. Lithograph. 66 × 52
Proceeds donated to the Prince Bernhard Foundation, Amsterdam.

77 *Tower Bridge* (ww 475)
Frontispiece to Jan Tomeš, *Oskar Kokoschka, Londoner Ansichten, Englische Landschaften*, published by F. Bruckmann, Munich, 1972. Standard edition of 200. Signed and dated in pencil *O Kokoschka 72*. Numbered *X/X*. Lithograph. 20 × 24·5

78 *The Women of Troy* (ww 476-490)
Four from the suite of 15 lithographs, drawn 1971–1972, and published by Marlborough Graphics, London, 1973. Standard edition of 50, plus 6 sets each with original drawing, and 10 sets for the artist. Each signed in pencil *O Kokoschka* and numbered *1/50*. Size of sheets 56 × 45·8
(1) *Hektor's helmet* * (ww 476)
(9) *Kassandra prophesies disaster* (ww 484)
for the victors
(10) *Kassandra is led away to Aga-* (ww 485)
memnon's ship
(15) *Hekuba turns away from burn-* (ww 490)
ing Troy

79 *Olda* (ww 491)
1972. Issued with the first and second de luxe editions of Kokoschka's *Erzählungen*, volume 2 of

Das Schriftliche Werk, edited by Heinz Spielmann and published by Hans Christians, Hamburg, 1974. Total edition of 159. From the first edition. Signed in pencil *O Kokoschka* and numbered *1/40*. Dry-point. 15·8 × 9·8

80 *Self-portrait* (ww 492)
1972. Issued with the first and second de luxe editions of Kokoschka's *Vorträge, Aufsätze, Essays*, volume 3 of *Das Schriftliche Werk*, edited by Heinz Spielmann and published by Hans Christians, Hamburg, 1975. Total edition of 160. From the first edition. Signed in pencil *O Kokoschka* and numbered *1/40*. Dry-point. 15·2 × 9·1

81 Oskar Kokoschka and Gottfried von Einem, *Die träumenden Knaben* (The Dreaming Youths), Cantata, Op. 41. Published by Boosey and Hawkes Ltd, London, 1972. Inscribed in pencil with the dedication from the author: *für den eifrigen Sammler von OK graf Bethusy zum Vergnügen*, and in ink from the composer: *Graf Bethusi-Huc diese Erstfassung mit herzlichem Dank und guten Wünschen Gottfried Einem 10/111/74*.
Gottfried von Einem was commissioned to set Kokoschka's lyrical prose poem (written in 1907 and first published by the Wiener Werkstätte in 1908) to music by Austrian Radio.

82 *His Beatitude Benedictos I Greek* (ww 495)
Orthodox Patriarch of Jerusalem *
No. 3 from the portfolio of six lithographs entitled *Jerusalem Faces*, drawn 1973, and published by Marlborough Graphics, Vaduz, and George Weidenfeld and Nicolson Ltd, London and Jerusalem, 1974. Standard edition of 150, plus 10 copies each signed by the artist and the sitter, and 20 proofs for the artist. Inscribed *Patriarch Benedicte*. 62 × 50
The portfolio was published for the benefit of the Jerusalem Foundation.

83 *Golda Meir II* (ww 499)
Drawn 1973 and published by Marlborough Graphics Ltd, Vaduz, and George Weidenfeld and Nicolson Ltd, London and Jerusalem, 1974. Standard edition of 150, plus 10 copies each signed by the artist and the sitter, and 20 proofs for the artist. Standard edition printed in sepia. Inscribed in ink on the back *For Bethusy-Huc from Barbara 8 May 75*. Lithograph, printed in black. 41·3 × 31·5
Drawn at the same time as the portrait of Golda Meir included in *Jerusalem Faces*, this portrait was published for the benefit of The Jerusalem Foundation also.

84 Portrait head of *Oskar Kokoschka*
By Karel Vogel (1897–1961). The clay model of 1934 was in the collection of Bohuslav Kokoschka, brother of Oskar. This bronze is the only one which he has permitted to be made. Bronze. 30 × 30

85 Portrait head of *Oskar Kokoschka* *
By Berta Patockova-Kokoschka, sister of Oskar. Probably made in 1962. Lettered *OBK*. Porcelain. 20 × 13

12 *Self-portrait*. 1966. Lithograph. (65)

13 *Die Eindringlinge* (The Intruders). Illustration to *Die chinesische Mauer*, 1914. Lithograph. (17)

14 *Adam and Eve*. Illustration to *Hiob*, 1917. Lithograph. (23)

15 *Max Reinhardt*. 1919. Lithograph. (29)

52

16 *Corona I*. 1919. Lithograph. (27)

17 *The Concert I*. 1921. Lithograph. (31)

18 *Trudl mit Strohhut* (Trudl with straw hat). 1931. Lithograph. (43)

19 *Ruth II*. 1922. Lithograph. (35)

20 *Olda Kokoschka*. 1949. Dry-point. (47)

21 *In Memory of the Children of Europe who have to die of cold and hunger this Xmas.* 1945.
Lithograph. (45)

22 *Saul and David: David in his old age*. 1969. Lithograph. (71·39)

23 *Hellas: Shepherd's Dog.* 1964. Lithograph. (59·I·11)

24 *The Women of Troy: Hektor's helmet.* 1973. Lithograph. (78·1)

25 *His Beatitude Benedictos I Greek Orthodox Patriarch of Jerusalem.* 1974. Lithograph. (82)

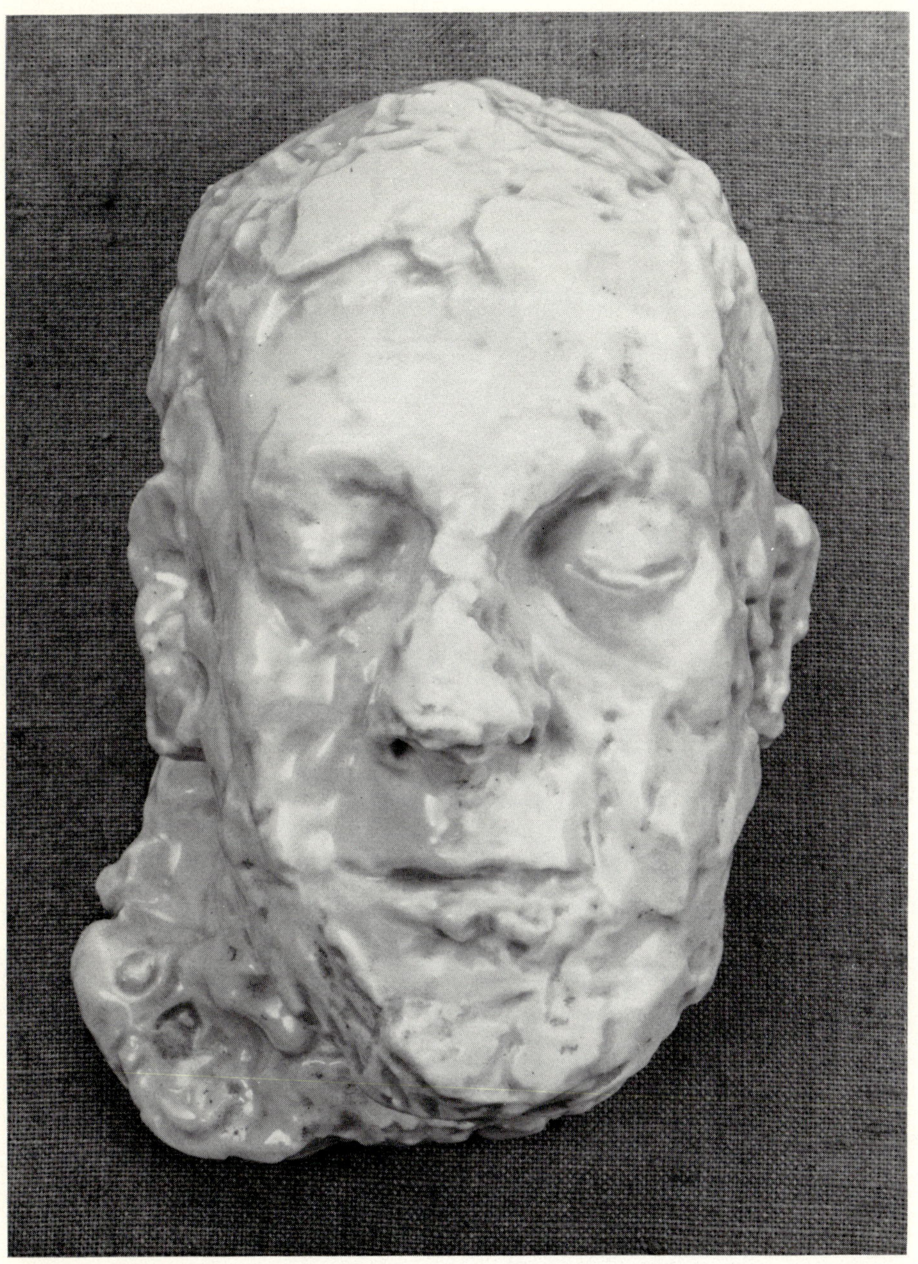

26 *Oskar Kokoschka* by Berta Patockova-Kokoschka. Porcelain. (85)

27 *Der Künstler und die Muse* (The artist and his Muse). 1922. Plaster. (34)

Printed in England for Her Majesty's Stationery Office by McCorquodale Printers Limited, London
HM 8527   Dd 327003   3M   4/76   McC 3339